THEOLOGIANS TODAY: F. X. DURRWELL

Other titles in the THEOLOGIANS TODAY series:

Hans Urs von Balthasar
Yves M. J. Congar, OP
Hans Küng
Henri de Lubac, SJ
Karl Rahner, SJ
Edward Schillebeeckx, OP
F. J. Sheed

THEOLOGIANS TODAY: a series selected and edited by Martin Redfern

F. X. DURRWELL, CSSR

SHEED AND WARD · LONDON AND NEW YORK

First published 1972
Sheed & Ward Inc, 64 University Place, New York, N.Y. 10003
and Sheed & Ward Ltd, 33 Maiden Lane, London WC2E 7LA

This selection © Sheed & Ward Ltd, 1972

Nihil obstat: John M. T. Barton, S.T.D., L.SS.
Imprimatur: ✠ Victor Guazzelli, V.G
Westminster, 19 April 1972

Library of Congress Catalog Number 72-2163

This book is set in 12/14 Monotype Imprint

Made and printed in Great Britain by
Billing & Sons Limited, Guildford and London

CONTENTS

Introduction	7
1. The Resurrection of Christ, Birth of the Church	9
2. The Sacrament of Scripture	59
3. The Mass in our Lives	83
4. Creation and the Apostolate	99

Sources and Acknowledgments

"The Resurrection of Christ, Birth of the Church" (1958) is from *The Resurrection: A Biblical Study*, London and New York, Sheed & Ward, 1960.

"The Sacrament of Scripture" and "The Mass in our Lives" (1960) are from *In the Redeeming Christ*, London and New York, Sheed & Ward, 1963.

"Creation and the Apostolate" (1970) is from *The Mystery of Christ and the Apostolate*, London and New York, Sheed & Ward, 1972.

INTRODUCTION

The last twenty-five years, and in particular the last ten years, have seen a remarkable flowering of Roman Catholic theology. But for the non-specialist—for the busy parish priest, the active layman, the student—the very wealth of this development presents a range of problems. With which theologian does he begin? Which theologians will he find the most rewarding? Can he ignore any of them?

There are no quick or final answers to such questions, of course, but I hope that this new *Theologians Today* series will help many Catholics to find their own answers more easily. It is designed to achieve two main purposes. Each individual book provides a short but representative introduction to the thought of an outstanding Catholic theologian of the present day, and the series as a whole demonstrates the kind of relationship existing between the best contemporary Catholic theology and official Church teaching.

Both purposes are met by the framework common to all the books. For each book I have selected—and arranged in order of original publication—four pieces which indicate the range in time, approach, and special interest of the theologian concerned. Partly to make my selections more 'objective', but mainly to emphasise the close connection between the theologian's writing and the teaching of Vatican II, I have keyed the articles to the four major documents of that Council—the four Constitutions, on the Church, on Revelation, on the Liturgy, and on the Church in the Modern World.

The selections are very much my own. The theologians themselves, or other editors, would doubtless have made different choices. Nevertheless, I feel that—granted my self-imposed limitations of space and conciliar theme, and the further necessary limitations imposed by copyright or by a proper preference for the out-of-print or inaccessible over the widely available—I have done my own best for men to whom I owe a large debt of gratitude.

The English translation of F. X. Durrwell's *The Resurrection* was published in 1960, and it had an immediate and lasting effect on the English-speaking Catholic world: it powerfully reasserted the centrality of the resurrection in Christian faith, and it gave great impetus to the revival of biblical study and theology. The first article here is a key section from that book, and the following articles from later books develop the same approach in particular fields.

MARTIN REDFERN

1. The Resurrection of Christ, Birth of the Church

"When Jesus rose up again after suffering death on on the cross for mankind, he manifested that he had been appointed Lord, Messiah, and Priest for ever, and he poured out on his disciples the Spirit promised by the Father. The Church, consequently, receives the mission to proclaim and to establish among all peoples the Kingdom of Christ and of God. It becomes on earth the initial budding forth of that Kingdom."—*Dogmatic Constitution on the Church*, I, 5.

In the prophecy of the Old Testament, as well as in Christ's teaching and the preaching of the Apostles, Christ's person is bound up with a reality which projects beyond it and yet forms one body with it. Scripture tries to define this entity and express the richness of it with magnificent phrases: "the People of God", the "Kingdom", "Temple", or "Church" of God, "the Body of Christ", "the Bride of Christ". Here I am presupposing the basic unity of this entity, despite its many varying titles and facets.

1. *The Date of the Church's Birth*

i. The Synoptics

Preserving the inheritance from the prophets that Christ's message contained, the Synoptics present the reality of the Messiah's coming in the framework of the Kingdom of God.

The teaching of the three Evangelists about the coming of that kingdom needs to be examined closely. Some parables, comparing the Kingdom to a seed, date the coming of the Kingdom from Christ's preaching. The entry of the Kingdom into the world follows upon the work of John the Baptist. He is the Precursor, the last of the Prophets sent to announce the Kingdom: from then on, the Kingdom makes its way into the world in power (Mt 11:12ff.); the coming into action of the Spirit of God and the flight of the devils are proof that it has come in triumph (Lk 9:20.)

Yet even at that moment the Kingdom appears to be a reality of the future. Our Lord declares that it is near, not that it is present: "The time is accomplished, and the Kingdom of God is at hand: repent and believe the good news." (Mk 1:15.) This was to be the theme of his preaching for some time. When Christ gives the Twelve a share in his ministry, he tells them to preach this message: "The Kingdom of God is at hand." (Mt 10:7.) Much later in his public life, he entrusts the same message to the seventy-two disciples. (Lk 10:9.) The Kingdom, then, is not established; on the eve of the Passion it is still awaited. (Lk 22:18.)

Our Lord had certainly told those who were to preach the Kingdom something about its coming, and they remained in expectation up till the end. They tried in advance to assure themselves places at the right and left hand of the King, when he came to the throne. (Mt 20:21.) For them the Kingdom was not yet inaugurated, for our Lord himself had not yet entered it. Their state of mind might well have been expressed in the words of the Good Thief: "Lord, remember me when thou shalt come into thy kingdom." (Lk 23:42; cf. Lk 19:11.)

The Resurrection of Christ

One must not therefore give too wide an interpretation to those texts which affirm the arrival of the Kingdom during Christ's life on earth. It would be surprising if John, in his prison, had remained a splendid lonely figure from the Old Testament, left outside the Kingdom (Mt 11:11) which publicans and harlots were able to enter. (Mt 21:31.) The Kingdom of God was present in Israel by its tangible, and already effective, proximity. "The Kingdom of Heaven is in your midst", declared our Lord. (Lk 17:21.) But this presence was to be followed by the real coming. The Pharisees had asked when it would come. Our Lord's reply was that the Kingdom was coming—was a reality of the future—but that one could not therefore say, "Behold here, or behold there" it is; its coming would not be observable at all, for it was already there in the midst of them. This context suggests that it was certainly present but present so far simply as a principle and a hope. The messianic climax that was to bring it into the world was still in the future. Thus the Kingdom would suddenly appear without it having been possible to foresee and watch its coming.

It was in Christ's person that that fundamental presence and that hope were contained, and in him that the Kingdom was suddenly to be revealed. The Spirit, by whom the Kingdom of God was to be imposed on the world, was already operative in Christ. (Lk 11:20.) The Kingdom was, as it were, incarnate in Christ, and its lot was linked with his. It came with Christ (Mk 11:10); to see the Son of

Man coming was to assist at the arrival of the Kingdom (cf. Mt 16:28 and Mk 10:9, Greek text); the words "Christ" and "Kingdom" seem interchangeable (cf. Mt 19:29 and Lk 18:29); by following the one one enters the other, and anyone rejected by Christ is by that very fact expelled from the Kingdom. (Mt 25:34ff.) "The least" in the Kingdom are identified with Christ, for he is the whole Kingdom.

Our Lord's coming on earth was not as yet a royal coming, and therefore the Kingdom remained a seed and a hope. In the mind of the Apostles, the inauguration of the Kingdom required the glorification of their Master: "Grant to us that we may sit one on thy right hand and the other on thy left hand, in thy glory", Mark quotes them as saying (Mk 10:37), while in Matthew, it is "in thy kingdom". (20:21). To them the Kingdom of God was that age of glory promised by the Prophets, which obsessed them as it obsessed the rest of the Jews. And those who, on the "holy mount", were privileged to contemplate Christ transfigured in "the excellent glory" (2 Pet 1:17), thought that the time had come. Their only doubt was how to reconcile this immediate establishment of the Kingdom with the teaching of the scribes that Elijah must first return. But our Lord broke into this circle of ideas to talk of his death: the inauguration of the kingdom which they are expecting soon and in splendour is to be preceded by the deepest humiliation; the entry into glory is to take place in a resurrection from the dead. (Mt 17:9-13.)

The Resurrection of Christ

Though Christ was not in accord with his disciples about the way in which it would come, he did at least share their expectancy. When setting out for the last time on the journey up to Jerusalem, while those around him were talking of the coming of the Kingdom, he compared himself to a nobleman going to take possession of a kingdom. (Lk 19:11ff.) The kingdom which he ruled was, then, not yet founded. When later on, he said, "Ought not Christ to have suffered these things and so to enter into his glory?" (Lk 24:26), we seem to catch an echo of that phrase so often used, that he must enter into his kingdom, an echo, and the fulfilment of an expectation.

The setting up of the Kingdom presupposes a display of power. That is why the driving out of demons "by the finger of God" was evidence that the Kingdom had, in a sense, come. (Lk 11:20.) But its true coming in power was to be later: "There are some of them that stand here, who shall not taste death, till they see the Kingdom of God coming in power." (Mk 8:39). It is not that the Kingdom will in itself be more powerful than at present, but simply that it will come, in the glory and power which characterize "the coming".

Christ told his judges that the prophecy of Daniel (7) was about to be realized. Hereafter they were to see the Son of Man coming on the clouds of heaven. (Mt 26:64.) Daniel had described both the foundation of a kingdom and the consecration of a king. After the world had seen the passing of the four earthly empires, whose characteristic features and ephemeral nature were symbolized by the four beasts, "one like the Son of Man came with the clouds of heaven". In this heavenly being the kingdom from above was inaugurated; at his coming "power and dominion and the glory of the kingdoms" were given "to the people of the saints". In the writer's mind, the messianic leader and his community were so closely linked and benefited so inseparably from the one kingship, that when the symbolism is explained (verses 18–27) we cannot distinguish between the king and his people—indeed, it is only the community of saints that is mentioned.

When our Lord unfolded this vision before his judges, he announced, as well as his own glorification, the inauguration of the Kingdom. Certainly the Gospel context specially emphasizes the individual significance of the Son of Man; yet this coming must be interpreted as the arrival of the Kingdom as well as of its king. The text does nothing to modify the meaning of the reference to Daniel which it suggests. They had asked our Lord if he were the Messiah. Yes, was his answer, and my kingdom is now beginning.

All these texts presuppose the idea of a kingdom incarnate in the person of our Lord, a kingdom revealed in Christ's own coming in triumph. Messianic kingdom and messiahship go together; the Kingdom is inaugurated at the moment when Christ enters upon the exercise of his messianic power.

A sombre parable coming only a few days before his death, the parable of the wicked husbandmen,

The Resurrection of Christ

leading into that of the cornerstone, also brackets the coming of the Kingdom with the glorification of our Lord.

Having said what the husbandmen did to their master's son, he asked: "What therefore will the lord of the vineyard do to them?" And his hearers replied, "He will destroy those husbandmen and will give the vineyard to others." And our Lord concluded, "Therefore I say to you, that the Kingdom of God shall be taken from you, and shall be given to a nation yielding the fruits thereof." At the time of our Lord's speaking, the Kingdom of Heaven set up on earth was still the theocracy of Israel, administered by the priests and scribes.

To let his opponents know what happened to the son who had been put to death, Christ left the parable of the vineyard and went on to another, that of the cornerstone. Then, "fixing his eyes upon them, Jesus said: What is this then that is written, The stone which the builders rejected, the same is become the head of the corner?"

The second image resumes where the first had left off, with the rejection of the son. The builders of the house, selecting their materials, had rejected a stone as unsuitable. God picked it up, and made it the "head of the corner" of his house.

This is more than just a symbol of the Resurrection. Christ was announcing the Kingdom founded upon his death, and inaugurated in his resurrection. The image of the house indicates a community of nations, and the stone the place the Son occupies in it, rejected by man and then chosen by God. In the first parable the husbandmen had plotted: "This is the heir, let us kill him, that the inheritance may be ours." The second parable, in contrast with the first, tells us how the son returns to his place as heir of the kingdom denied him by the Jews.

On the eve of his death, our Lord "sat down at table and the twelve Apostles with him. And he said to them: With desire I have desired to eat this pasch with you, before I suffer. For I say to you, that from this time I will not eat it, till it be fulfilled in the Kingdom of God. And having taken the chalice, he gave thanks, and said: Take and divide it among you; For I say to you, that I will not drink of the fruit of the vine till the Kingdom of God come." (Lk 22:14–18.)

Even as late as this, then, the Kingdom of God was still a reality of the future; our Lord said it was to come (Lk 22:18), and the old institutions which prefigured it were still in force. (22:16.) But from thenceforward, our Lord would not eat that Pasch again until its fulfilment in the Kingdom; he would not again taste wine till the Kingdom was come. The Kingdom was in sight; never before had Christ spoken of it as so close. He took leave of the ancient paschal rite which was to be "fulfilled" by a new reality in the coming Kingdom.

Matthew (26:29) and Mark (14:25) place the Kingdom of God in the far-off eschatological future; the "new wine" to be drunk there suggests a drink that will elate the feasters at a mysterious table. But

The Resurrection of Christ

in Luke, the kingdom is close and of this world; its coming is linked with that of the Eucharist, and in the Evangelist's mind, the institution of the Eucharist inaugurates the true pasch of the Kingdom. "From now on, we get in Luke a suggestion of something other than a purely eschatological banquet in this Kingdom of God . . . It instantly suggests that sphere into which the new paschal rite opens out, the Church." The birth of that Church was very near.

The words Christ said when he passed the chalice round at the supper, according to Luke, make it quite clear that the Church was to be born between this meal and Christ's appearances after the Resurrection: "I will not drink of the fruit of the vine till the Kingdom of God come." (22:18.) Luke does not speak of any sublime fulfilment of the pasch in the world to come; he purposely changes the text given by Mark and leaves out the mysterious new wine. He was declaring simply that this is the last time Christ would taste wine on earth before his messianic consummation. "In allowing us to understand that Christ will eat and drink again in the Kingdom, he was no doubt simply thinking of the meals that were to take place after the Resurrection." Christ would once again eat with his disciples on earth in his new life (Lk 24:30, 42–3; Acts 1:4), and drink with them (Acts 10:41), and St. Luke is alone in emphasizing these meals. In his mind the inauguration of the Kingdom was to be placed between the paschal supper and the appearances of the risen Christ. Luke thus teaches us that the Kingdom had not yet come, but that it was very close and was to be inaugurated before Christ returned to his Apostles.

The image Christ used to announce the Kingdom explains both the delay and the nearness. Isaiah (25:6–7) had foretold for "that day" an abundant feast for the nations on Mount Zion. The favourite symbol in rabbinical literature to describe the Kingdom was that of a banquet. Our Lord had used it in many different forms (Mt 5:6; 8:11; 22:1ff.; 25:10; 26:29; Lk 12:37; 15:23; 22:15–18, 29f.); now, in this supreme moment, he returned to it: "I will drink no more of the fruit of the vine until that day when I shall drink it new in the Kingdom of God."

Christ certainly did not identify the Kingdom with this joyful banquet in so many words. But a meal taken in the Kingdom must in fact be the one he had so often spoken of, and which was the Kingdom itself.

Though the words open up an eschatological perspective, the banquet was not relegated to some distance in the future; placed by Christ in the framework of the mystery, it could begin at once. Thus Luke has taken it upon himself to interpret this Kingdom of the Church on earth, and he places here the commands given to those whom Christ put at the head of his Church, which close with the words: "I dispose to you as my father has disposed to me a kingdom, that you may eat and drink at my table in my kingdom." (Lk 22:25–30.)

But Christ gave an unexpected deepening to the

image: the messianic banquet was a paschal meal: "I will not eat this pasch again till it be fulfilled in the Kingdom of God." (Lk 22:16.)

In the Old Testament, the whole nation gathered in the sacrificial sharing of the paschal lamb, symbol of the national community, bond of its unity and expression of its sacred character. (cf. Ex 12:43–9.) The new Kingdom in its turn was to consist of feasters at a sacred table, of the totality of those who communicate with Christ in the true sacrifice of the Lamb.

To his hearers, already imbued with the mystical doctrine of a meal shared round God's table, the image was a striking one; it suggested intimacy with God and an indestructible brotherhood, sealed by the sacred food, among the banqueters; as a paschal meal, it spoke of a joyful deliverance and a land flowing with milk and honey.

The paschal meal involved the immolation of the lamb. In Luke, with the promise of the Pasch's being "fulfilled", followed by the institution of the Eucharist, Christ was indicating that he himself was the victim "delivered for us". Our food at the meal, he was yet also to be our fellow-banqueter in the fulfilment of the Pasch (22:16), he was to eat and drink in joy at the table of his own sacrifice. The disciples would eat and drink with him, in the joy of their paschal deliverance, being nourished by him. The people of the Kingdom would be all those who communicate in the true Pasch.

In the former series of texts, the Kingdom was to

be born as soon as Christ was glorified, his death being the condition of his glorification. But here, the death itself comes into the mystery of the Kingdom, and yet it is in glory that the Kingdom unfolds, for the feast of the immolated lamb is celebrated in the joy of the new wine, and the Saviour, having passed through death, takes part in it. Here, more than anywhere, the Kingdom is identified with Christ; the disciples enter it by taking part in a meal in which Christ gives himself to them, in his immolation and in his glory.

The texts which date the inauguration of the Kingdom from the glorification of Christ present that kingdom as an other-worldly reality, belonging to the divine sphere, in the clouds of heaven. But the Kingdom's history includes a previous, earthly phase, when it is subject to human organization, and governed by the Master's stewards, by Peter and the rest of the Twelve, who are set over the household to give them their measure of wheat in due season (Lk 12:42.) Though it is earthly in a human sense, it is already the Kingdom of heaven, a reality of the other world introduced into the existence of this one. Matthew's gospel applies the term "Church" to the Kingdom in this phase (Cf. 16:18, 19.)

But the Kingdom did not exist even in this earthly form before Christ's death. At Caesarea Philippi, our Lord promised Peter that he would build his Church upon him and give him its keys. It was a declaration and a promise; the building and the giving were to come later. Matthew notes (16:21ff.) that from then on our Lord began to speak of the necessity of his dying and rising again. It is indeed a noteworthy fact that the two prophecies come together.

Thus the inauguration of the Kingdom did not precede Christ's death, but was identified with his entering into glory. The messianic explosion, so to say, from which the Kingdom had to rise, took place in Christ himself; the Kingdom opened in him.

ii. The Acts

After the Resurrection, Christ appeared to the Apostles for forty days, "speaking of the Kingdom of God". (Acts 1:3.) The time had come, thought the disciples: "Wilt thou at this time restore again the Kingdom to Israel?" (1:6). Our Lord rectified their ideas, directing their thoughts to a spiritual kingdom, marked by the presence of the Spirit: "You shall receive the power of the Holy Ghost coming upon you."

From Pentecost on, the Apostles had seen, before St Paul, and more keenly than he, "in the resurrection of Christ and the descent of the Holy Spirit, the beginnings of the Kingdom of God." (Cerfaux.)

St Peter was the first to give the great news. He proclaimed the arrival of Christ at the throne of David, his father, at the right hand of God (Acts 2:31–6). He told Christ's enemies that the prophecy made long ago about them was now fulfilled: "Jesus Christ of Nazareth, whom you crucified, whom God had raised from the dead . . . This is the stone which was rejected by you the builders, which is become the head of the corner." (4:10–11.) The leaders of the house of Israel had tossed Christ aside as a stone that was unusable, but God had taken that stone up again and made it the corner-stone, the principle of strength and cohesion for the whole building.

The outpouring of the Spirit was the proof that Christ was thus exalted (2:33) and that the Kingdom of God had begun.

iii. St John

In the Synoptics Christ sums up prophetic tradition about the Kingdom and brings it to its conclusion.

St John gives us a saying of Christ's more in line with the liturgical nature of the fourth gospel, which completes a different tradition.

Prophecy had foretold the building of a temple with perfect proportions (Ezek 40–42), on a Mount Zion raised up higher than all other mountains (Isa 2:2), to be most holy (Ezek 43:12; 45:3–4), forever enveloped in Yahweh's cloud of glory (Is 4:5), for God was to dwell in it forever (Ezek 37:26–8); a receptacle of mysterious riches, a river was to flow out from under its gate to irrigate the desert and bring life to the Dead Sea. (Ezek 47:1–12; Joel 4:18.) The Temple will stand in the midst of the people forever, to sanctify them and show that they are holy. (Ezek 37:28.)

This expectation is easily understandable in the light of the tremendous importance, both as symbol and as reality, which the Temple held in national and religious life. It was inconceivable that the messianic

The Resurrection of Christ

kingdom, crowning the ancient theocracy, should not have a Temple in Jerusalem whose glory should be proportionate to that of the Kingdom itself. Their hope was based on the firm foundation of God's word. Nathan had promised David that a Messiah should spring from his seed, and should build a house to Yahweh. (2 Kings 7:13.) When the prophecies about God's kingdom received their first hint of fulfilment with the return from exile, Zerubbabel, who raised the Temple from its ruins, saw some of the messianic praises applied to him. (Zech. 3:8; 6:12.)

Daniel had rather hazily foreseen a new institution in the messianic future which he tried to express by the image of the sanctuary, having first represented it by the symbol of the Son of Man: "Seventy weeks are counted . . . that vision and prophecy may be fulfilled, and the saint of saints may be anointed." (9:24.)

When Christ, with some cords knotted into a scourge, drove out the merchants, the priests in charge of the Temple arrangements, who benefited from the business carried on there, asked him "What sign dost thou show unto us, seeing thou dost these things?" And our Lord replied: "Destroy this temple, and in three days I will raise it up." The Jews then said, "Six and forty years was this temple in building; and wilt thou raise it up in three days?" But he was talking of his body. (Jn 2:18–21.)

When ordered by the Jews to show the evidence of his power, our Lord answered: "Destroy this temple and I will rebuild it." That was his proof. The sanctuary the Jews were going to destroy was their temple of stone, the one the argument logically suggested. They were angry that this layman should assume power over the House of God. Unless there was a gesture to indicate that he meant his body, which seems unlikely, the answer remains a total enigma if "this temple" was not the temple under discussion. The Evangelist's reflexion, "he spoke of the temple of his body", explains the second part of the answer, which seems to make nonsense—"In three days I will raise it up"—and which was what the Jews objected to: "Six and forty years . . . and wilt thou raise it up in three days?"

This was brought up as a charge against Christ at his trial: "We heard him say, I will destroy this temple made with hands, and within three days I will build another not made with hands." (Mk 14:58.) The Evangelist points out that it was a false witness, but he does not therefore mean to contest "the authenticity of the saying—its very strangeness puts it beyond any possible doubt. The false witness turned on to the revolutionary construction put upon a very mysterious utterance." (Grandmaison.)

"It would seem that the witnesses were not wrong in contrasting a temple built by hands and a temple not built by hands." (Huby.) Unless we are to look on Mark's text as a later Christian development, the contrast between a material and a spiritual temple must come from Christ.

A similar charge was brought against the deacon

The Resurrection of Christ

Stephen: "This man ceaseth not to speak words against the Holy Place and the Law. We have heard him say, that this Jesus of Nazareth shall destroy this place, and shall change the traditions which Moses delivered unto us." (Acts 6:13-14.) The accusation was not without foundation. His discourse before the Sanhedrin closed with the declaration that God does not dwell in temples made by the hand of man. (Acts 7:48.) The Spirit had given this Hellenistic Christian the work of cutting a path out of the Mosaic system for the Christian community. He had the soul of a Paul, but a younger Paul than the one we know in the Epistles. He had no fear of proclaiming the abolition of the Mosaic institutions and the forthcoming destruction of the Temple, and so interpreting our Lord's prophecy.

The Jews were taking it upon themselves to destroy their temple. The Christ of flesh was the keystone of the old order. Take away the keystone and the house will collapse. At the moment of Christ's death, the veil of the Temple was rent from top to bottom. The material destruction bore witness in the eyes of the world to the spiritual.

To take the place of the temple of stone, the body of Christ was built up in the Resurrection. Up till then the Lord God had dwelt amid his people in that temple of stone. There he held court, "sitting upon the cherubims" (1 Sam 4:4), surrounded by angelic hymns of praise. (Is 6:1-3.) There on the holy hill was the point of contact at which the prayers and sacrifices of the people came to the Lord, where

Yahweh was revealed to those who believed in him, and invited them to communicate at his table.

The Temple was the source and guarantee of the people's unity. When Israel gathered before the tabernacle of reunion, or in the court of the Temple, they were conscious that the bond linking them to Yahweh made them one, and whenever they sat down to table with God at the sacrificial meal, the bonds uniting them became closer.

Three days after his death, Christ became, in his body, the new Temple, the dwelling place of the glory, the place of the divine revelation, the point of contact between God and his people, and the bond uniting the people together. He was to be the house of prayer and praise where the people would gather, where they would worship together in the odour of sacrifice and sit down to table with God. But in this temple not made with hands, worship would be offered in spirit and in truth.

Alongside the idea of the messianic temple St John also mentions the Kingdom of God. Our Lord declared to Nicodemus that "unless a man be born again of water and the Holy Ghost he cannot enter the Kingdom of God". (Jn 3:5.) Exegetes no longer believe that baptism with water and the Holy Ghost came before the Resurrection. It was Christ in glory who set in motion the economy of the Spirit. (7:39.) Man's birth as a citizen of the Kingdom cannot be separated from Christ's entry into glory, and until that entry, the Kingdom was not established on earth.

For this evangelist of Christ the Lamb (1:29;

The Resurrection of Christ

19:36; Rev *passim*), the mystery of the Kingdom can be expressed in terms of a flock. (10.) Christ is its leader. It seems as though this flock existed before the Passion, with Christ on earth walking at its head, awaiting only the reunion in the fold of Israel of the "other sheep". It is usual with the Christ of John's gospel, conscious of the riches of salvation he possesses, to anticipate his life of glory. Certainly the sheep are beginning to gather round their shepherd: the parable came on the occasion of the Jewish leaders casting out a sheep of the flock of Israel, the man born blind, whom Christ took among his own sheep, declaring that he did not lead his flock astray. Yet his gaze was going beyond the reality of the present. The flock he described was already, without prejudice to his own unique leadership, led by other shepherds who came and went in Christ. But the Apostles had not yet received their shepherds' crooks (Jn 21:15–17). Our Lord was in fact speaking of a reality of the future. The thought of his death and resurrection hovers over the whole allegory (10:15, 17). The flock was still in an imperfect state, penned within the enclosure of the old economy; other sheep were wandering outside that enclosure (10:16); our Lord must die and rise again to bring them into the unity of a flock which has no barriers of nationality.

On Palm Sunday, while the multitude crowded round Christ, some pagan proselytes tried to come to him. (Jn 12:20–33.) They said to Philip: "Sir, we would see Jesus." This was something unprecedented, and the Apostles deliberated together and laid the matter before their Master. Like the question put by the priests after he had driven out the merchants from the Temple, this overture from the Greeks suddenly opened a great vista to our Lord's mind. He saw the Gentiles crowding round him, and a wave of joy broke over him: "The hour is come, that the Son of Man should be glorified." But the thought of his triumph brought with it that of his death, which came so powerfully upon him that he was filled with an anguish of agony. He remembered that for his work to bear fruit he must first die: "Unless the grain of wheat falling into the ground die, itself remaineth alone. But if it die, it bringeth forth much fruit." In the Church's symbolism, beside the true vine stands this humbler image of the ear of wheat laden to bending point. It is a simple parable, but the essential teaching is the same as if it were an allegory. Christ is like the seed dying that it may be multiplied; when he is born again out of the tomb, he will no longer be one, but many, a laden ear born out of the sacrificed seed.

iv. The Symbolism of Events

As we study the Gospels more deeply, we come to perceive the word of God not only in what Christ said, but in everything he did and in all the circumstances of his life. By failing to advert to this, one is letting part of the priceless seed fall upon stones. A great many of the miracles are a kind of mime of what is taught by his words. Our Lord multiplies the loaves, and announces that he will give the bread of

The Resurrection of Christ

heaven; the walking on the water demonstrates the marvellous nature of his body, which is going to be given as food; he declares that he is the Light, and heals a blind man; he says he is the Resurrection and brings Lazarus back to life. The story of the Passion, above all, is rich in happenings which seem so arranged by God as to be a commentary upon it. John more than any of the others, is aware of this symbolism. When Judas left the upper room, "it was night". The innocent Christ was condemned, while Barabbas was acquitted. He was taken out of the gate; Simon was made to carry the cross behind our Lord. On either side of him criminals were crucified; one of the robbers goes into the Kingdom the other is determined to remain outside. The bones of the Lamb are not broken; a stroke of the lance causes blood and water to flow from his side, and, in the Jews' temple, the veil is rent. Each of these facts conceals a mystery, and the New Testament writers show more than once how struck they are by their symbolism. (Lk 20:15; Heb 13:12; Jn 19:35ff.; 1 Jn 5:8; Heb 10:20; Mt 16:24.)

Even coincidences in time can sometimes be significant. It is noteworthy that according to the Synoptics Christ ate the Pasch before his passion, whereas in John the priests did not immolate the paschal lamb until the evening of Good Friday. Strange though this double piece of information may seem, it can hardly be called in question, for upon so essential a point neither the information of the Synoptics, nor the accuracy of John's memory could be at fault. The fact that Christ and the Jewish priests celebrated the paschal meal at two different dates is best explained by a difference in reckoning which divided the nation; similar cases found in rabbinical writings support this suggestion. This unlikely fact fitted in well with Christ's design. The eating of the lamb with his Apostles marked out the Eucharist and the whole messianic banquet as a sacrificial and paschal meal. By coinciding with the immolation of the lambs in the Temple, Christ's immolation stands out as that of the true Lamb.

This placing of the acts of our redemption in the chronological pattern of the rites which typified them suggests that there must be a reason for the three days between Christ's death and resurrection. No doubt God's plan here was primarily an apologetic one: the genuineness of the death, duly recorded on Calvary, could be open to no doubt after three days in the tomb. But the choice of the third day seems also directed towards illustrating the mystery of the Resurrection as redeeming us, just as the coincidence with the immolation of the lamb expressed the mystery of the death.

The barley ripened about the time of the pasch. After the feast, "the next day after the sabbath", the children of Israel had to bring the first sheaf to Yahweh for a holocaust. (Lev 23:10–14.) The harvest then began. Thus, early in the morning the first Sunday after Christ's death, the priests would be offering to God the first-fruits collected from the other side of the Cedron. That same morning, Christ rose, the first sheaf of a different harvest. St. Paul seems to hint at this. (1 Cor 15:20.) The parable of the grain changing into the ear is now fulfilled and the harvest has begun. The first sheaf is consecrated by fire, and the whole harvest will be holy (Rom 11:16); the new people is now a religious reality, consecrated in the fire of the Spirit.

The fact that the Resurrection took place on the first day of the week is not without its mystery, if we read the Book of Revelation. Christian history as a separate entity began on a Sunday (Rev 1:10) with the appearance of the risen Christ, and will develop in a sevenfold cycle until it is completed in an endless sabbatical rest. The history of the new creation started on this first day of the week.

v. St Paul

The idea of the Church attains the dimensions proper to it in the theology of St Paul. The development of his thought and terminology continued up to the Epistles of the Captivity where it reached its highest point. Here his definition of the Church and her relationship with Christ receives its perfect formulation: "He [God] hath given him [Christ] as head over all the Church, which is his body." (Eph 1:22f.)

The two halves of this statement give the framework for our examination into the date of the Church's birth. Two questions present themselves: At what moment did Christ become head of the Church? And is the body of Christ with which the Church is identified the body of the risen Saviour?

Theologians Today: F. X. Durrwell

(*a*) *The Christ of Easter, Head of the Church.* The first chapter of the Epistle to the Ephesians enumerates the effects of the omnipotent force at work in the Resurrection, "that you may know . . . what is the exceeding greatness of his power towards us . . . which he wrought in Christ, raising him up from the dead . . . And he hath subjected all things under his feet, and hath given him as head over all the Church, which is his body . . ." (1:19–23.) The first effect of this raising power is the establishment of Christ as lord over all things. This first exaltation is completed in another. When everything is placed under the feet of the risen Christ, he is given to the Church as her head. All his glorification is directed towards this headship; in it the power of the Resurrection receives its crown.

The intimate union between the Church and Christ in his corporeal humanity makes it possible for Paul, later in the epistle, to exhort husbands and wives to take that relationship as their model: "Women, be subject to your husbands, as to the Lord; because the husband is the head of the wife, as Christ is the head of the Church, the saviour of his body." (Eph 5:22f.) Before becoming head of the Church, he had to win it for himself by saving it: he who is its Saviour is its Head. "It is to this saving and redeeming action that he owes his headship of the Church." (Huby.) His function as head crowns his function as redeemer.

But the very next verse seems to go against this conclusion: "Husbands, love your wives, as Christ also loved the Church, and delivered himself up for it; that he might sanctify it, cleansing it by the laver of water in the word of life." (5:25f.) It was, then, his love as husband which impelled Christ to die for his Church, and being husband is equivalent to being head. The bridge already existed, therefore, and Christ died for her.

It is not a valid objection. The metaphor of the bride conjures up a Church which existed before her espousals, and in this it is an imperfect metaphor. Christ's love of the Church was a love directed towards a future reality, a bridge created by his love. He delivered himself for her, so as to make ready "a laver of water" from which she was to emerge spotless and glorious, and at that moment he would unite himself to her. "We might think that St Paul, instead of using the original word, 'baptism' had chosen this expression, 'laver of water', to allude to the Greek marriage ceremonies, with special reference to the most important prenuptial religious rite—the bathing of the betrothed girl." (Huby.) Having purified her, Christ has presented himself to his bride (5:27) and united himself to her in her flawless beauty. The heroic sacrifice of love came before Christ's real and living union with his Church, and before that union, the Church as such did not exist all all. His bride's life began as the act of the Redemption was completed, in the Resurrection (cf. Eph 1:20ff.), when the "laver of water in the word of life" came to receive its complete symbolism and effectiveness.

Theologians Today: F. X. Durrwell

The Epistle to the Colossians is concerned to establish Christ's primacy over all things; it makes the Saviour's lordship a thing of cosmic dimensions. St Paul does this only to make clear the width of Christ's redemptive mission. Having indicated Christ's place as keystone of the universe, he considers him in his primacy over the Church: "And he is the head of the body, [that is] the Church." His right to be head stems from his being the principle, the firstborn from the dead, that in all things he may hold the primacy"; and finally, the reason for this primacy over the cosmos and the Church . . . "because in him it hath well pleased the Father that all fullness should dwell." (Col 1:18–19.)

His role as head of the Church stems from the fact that he is the principle. What does this mean? From the fact that he is the first, heading the procession of all who are to be raised from the dead. Better still, because the totality of the divine power of life is concentrated in him, "for in him it hath pleased the Father that all fullness should dwell." All the fullness of life and of God's sanctifying power is gathered up in the body of Christ. (Col 1:19; 2:9.) In Pauline theology this dynamic Christ can only be the risen Saviour.

St Paul works out his thought for us: this Christ-principle is the firstborn from the dead. He is the head because he is the first in the victory, first in time (1 Cor 15:23), but also in rank; in him life wins its supreme triumph; above all, he is first by the supremacy of his purpose: his resurrection opens the

The Resurrection of Christ

way to life for mankind. (1 Cor 15:45.) The word "first-born" of itself carries no such wealth of meaning, but the Apostle confers it. The first-born is the source and fullness of the life of the Church: "He hath given him as head over the Church, he . . . the firstborn from the dead."

According to this same epistle, Christian life in all its stages, even on earth, is a resurrection; the Church is an assembly of those who were dead and have risen again. (Col 2:12; 3:1–3.) The phrase "first-born from the dead" expresses "under a slightly different aspect the same concept of Christ as head of the body of the Church".

The Christ of glory, head of the Church, also appears as the eldest brother of a great family whose Father is God (Rom 8:29), or the founder of a new race quite different from the race of Adam, the Christian people. This humanity is rooted "in Christ" as in its native soil. We may therefore say that it is born in the Christ of glory, for the phrase *in Christo* is reserved to the risen Saviour.

As the father of mankind reborn, Christ receives the title of the new Adam. This honour is due both to his obedience, and to his life-giving action.

In the Epistle to the Romans (5:12–21), the second Adam is contrasted with the first because of his obedience. Whereas mankind, in the past, was condemned by pride to sin and death, Christ by his death of obedience has brought them new life in justice: "As by the disobedience of one man, many were made sinners, so by the obedience of one, many shall be made just." (5:19.) Yet even in this epistle, the merit of submission is not the only reason for calling Christ the new Adam. The new life, before being given to men, is in Christ himself; it is "a gift [of God] in the grace of one man". (5:15.) Because of his death, our Lord was able to give a life of grace, just as disobedience had first polluted the whole of human nature at its source. For the first man to become the father of a sinful humanity, he had not only to sin, but to beget; and Christ had not only to be obedient, but to communicate the life which his obedience had won.

The parallel between the two heads of the human race is completed, in this, by the First Epistle to the Corinthians: "Thus it is written: The first man Adam was made into a living soul; the last Adam into a quickening spirit . . . The first man was of the earth, earthly, the second came from heaven. Such as is the earthly, such also are the earthly; and such as is the heavenly, such also are they that are heavenly. Therefore, as we have borne the image of the earthly, let us bear also the image of the heavenly." (15:45–9.)

To the question: "How do the dead rise again? or with what manner of body shall they come?", the Apostle replies that there are two principles of life: our common ancestor, and Christ; and that there are two ways of life corresponding to them. From the first Adam we get our earthly and mortal life, from the second, a heavenly way of living in a spiritualized humanity.

The Resurrection of Christ

It is not an antithesis between two moral acts whereby the first man deserved to transmit mortality, and the second a divine life; it is simply a question of the principle animating them and enabling each to beget—the one to death, the other to immortality. Here the second Adam is not Christ dying in the weakness of the flesh, but the Man of Heaven, who has reached the peak of his divine life in the Resurrection, and who, unlike our ancestor in the flesh, begets us to the life of glory.

On the Cross the submission which atones and merits was completed; in the Resurrection Christ gives new life in the Holy Spirit. The first man and woman, by their disobedience, were reduced to the "carnal" state in which they could pass on to us only a life marked out for death; similarly, his obedience has established the second Adam in the "spiritual" state in which he can pass on to us the life of justification. Once our brother in Adam because of his carnal humanity, Christ has now become our father in the newness of his life of glory.

Henceforth, Christ appears with "the children whom God has given him". (Heb 2:13.) But his fatherhood is closer than that of our ancestor in the flesh. Adam, man of dust, was only the first link in the chain of generations leading to us; he lived only his own life, being simply "a living soul"; the "heavenly man" is a "living spirit" who begets us directly by animating us with his own life.

Out of the old humanity, God chose a holy people, to be an outline of the Church, but remaining, in its make-up, still in the sphere of Adam, an earthly and carnal reality. Membership of that people was guaranteed by a mark of the same nature in the flesh. To his new people God applies a circumcision too, but Christian rather than Mosaic: "It is in him too that you have been circumcised with a circumcision not made by the hand of man; by the despoiling of the body of flesh, by the circumcision of Christ, having been buried with him in baptism, you are risen in him and with him by faith in the power of God who has raised him from the dead. And whereas you were dead by your sins and the uncircumcision of your flesh, God has made you live again with Christ, forgiving you all your sins." (Col 2:11-13.)

The expression "in him" makes it clear from the beginning that the seal of membership in the new people is imprinted upon the believer by a sharing in the risen life of Christ. This circumcision is not just a small excision made in the flesh, but "the despoiling of the body of flesh". The operation is performed in baptism, which brings us into the death and resurrection of our Saviour. By this despoiling of the flesh, we share in the death of Christ, yet this putting to death of the carnal being is the result of our union with our Saviour's life: "Whereas you were dead . . . by the uncircumcision of your flesh [this symbolizes the carnal state] God has made you live again in Christ." Before being raised with Christ, they were in the uncircumcision of flesh, and therefore dead; "the circumcision of Christ", imprinted upon us by sharing in the resurrection of Christ, has

The Resurrection of Christ

come to put an end to the flesh.

This contrast between the two Adams places the risen Christ at the head of a new race of men. The contrast between the two circumcisions makes a parallel between this Christian humanity and the people of God gathered round their tabernacle, thus pinpointing the ecclesiastical nature of the new people.

From both points of view, the Church depends upon the Resurrection, for it was then that Christ, first man of the new creation, received the life of heaven in the death of his flesh, the circumcision of the Holy Ghost, and became both father of a new race, and head of the new People of God.

(b) The Glorified Body of Christ, Principle of the Church. It is not only as its Head that Christ is related to the Church. Even in the Synoptics there are the beginnings of an identification between our Lord and his kingdom. St Paul accentuates this identification and declares that the Church is actually the body of Christ. What body is it? Is it our Saviour's own body? If so, the mystery of Easter must have an influence upon the Church, for it affects Christ in his "bodiliness".

The identification between the Church and the body of Christ is not made equally strictly everywhere. The Church is first of all described as one describes a body, rather than actually defined as the body of Christ, and it is a description dominated by the metaphor of the head and members making up a single body with varying functions. In Hellenistic times, the comparison of civil society with the human body had become a commonplace. We might be hearing the fable of Aesop, as Menenius Agrippa recounted it to the Roman populace, when Paul uses it to show the usefulness of the varying *charismata* in the Church: "The body also is not one member, but is made up of many . . . If they all were one member, where would be the body? There are many members indeed, yet one body . . . The eye cannot say to the hand: I need not thy help; nor again the head to the feet: I have no need of you." (1 Cor. 12:14-21; cf. Rom 12:3-8.)

But whereas the Greek metaphor supposes a simple moral union among the members of a society, St Paul bases his exhortation on the real identification of Christians with the body of Christ, and puts forward the fable because of that identification: "As the body is one, and hath many members, and all the members of the body, whereas they are many, yet are one body, so also is Christ [one, and possesses many members]." The faithful are thus united to Christ as the members to the body. He continues: "For in one Spirit were we all baptized into one body [that of Christ], whether Jews or Gentiles, whether bond or free." (1 Cor 12:12f.) All you who are baptized are consecrated to the body of Christ, and hence Christ is one body possessing many members. "You are the body of Christ [united and identified with him in his body], and, individually, his members." (1 Cor 12:27.) Hence this definition: "The Church, which is his body." (Eph 1:22f; Col 1:18, 24.)

Nowadays we call the Church the mystical body of Christ, and to many people, the expression means no more than a social group, organized and united like a body, with Christ as its head. St Paul's meaning is more literal. He is not comparing the Church with a body, nor does he merely say that it is *a* body; it is the body of Christ, identified, not the least metaphorically, with the physical body of our Lord. The Church is the body of Christ because it is united, in all its believers, to the risen body of its Saviour.

The Pauline idea is not precisely the same as our conception of the body. The Semitic mind has a more comprehensive intuition of human nature, and does not separate the body from the principle that gives it life and is expressed through it. Hence St Paul can use a personal pronoun for the body (1 Cor 12:13; Gal 3:27), because it is extended to mean the whole human person. "So also ought men to love their wives as their own bodies. He that loveth his wife, loveth himself." (Eph 5:28.) Belonging to the body of Christ is therefore synonymous with belonging to Christ himself. (1 Cor 6:13f.; 2 Cor 4:10f.) However, the accent remains on the material element; the field of vision only extends beyond the body in its material nature in the body's own perspective. The body may designate the whole man, but only because the human being is present and expresses himself in his "bodiliness". "The Church is the body of Christ, meaning Christ's corporeal being, Christ himself as existing corporeally." (Malevez.) To be the body of Christ means, therefore, to be "in Christ", but in a bodily Christ. And conversely, to be in Christ is to belong to his body.

The Church's union with Christ's body gives Paul a motive for exhorting us to respect our own bodies: "Know you not that your bodies are the members of Christ? Shall I then take the members of Christ and make them the members of a harlot? God forbid. Or know you not that he who is joined to a harlot is made one body with her? For it is said: They two shall be in one flesh. But he who is joined to the Lord is one spirit." (1 Cor 6:15–17.)

Because he always sees man as a unity, the Apostle can say not merely that the faithful are members of Christ, but that their bodies are members of Christ. Even in his material being, the Christian is a member of Christ, and it is of Christ in his physical being that we are members in our bodies. Furthermore, the parallel he puts forward between the two unions—with Christ and with the harlot—demands that we be quite literal in understanding the body of Christ to which we are united. "It is the union of a physical body with another physical body which is in question in the mention of intercourse with a prostitute, and to this Paul opposes union with the body of Christ as an antithesis." (Cerfaux.) The union is an absolutely real one, and Christ is thought of as a corporeal being.

Paul concludes: "He who is joined to the Lord is one spirit." One would have expected him to say, "He who is joined to the Lord becomes one body

The Resurrection of Christ

with him." They are two ways of expressing the same thought. The body of Christ is "spiritual", our union with it is in the order of the spirit, and the faithful are one spirit by being that body. (Eph 4:4.) The change to "one spirit" suggested itself to the apostle as opposed to the union in "one flesh".

In the Epistle to the Ephesians (5:22–33), the apostle once again works out these same ideas of the union in a single body of man and woman, of Christ and the Church. This time they are not placed in antithesis, but provide a comparison on which to base an exhortation on the relationship between Christian husbands and wives: "Women", he urges, "be subject to your husbands as to the Lord: because the husband is the head of the wife as Christ is the head of the Church, the saviour of the body." (5:22.) The image of the head suggests pre-eminence and the right to command; it would fit in with a purely moral union connecting the Church to Christ by social bonds. But from this starting-point, the Apostle's thought takes a very definite line; the union of marriage seems to him more than a moral one, and the relationship between Christ and the Church is formed in a single physical body: ". . . Christ is the head of the Church, who is the saviour of the body". The argument implies the idea that, parallel with the Church as Christ's body, the wife is the husband's body. The role of "head" adds to this idea of one body the further note of an authority vested in Christ and in the husband.

He does not suggest to husbands that they make

use of their right to command, but recommends their special duty of love and devotion. He returns to the example of Christ and the Church, recalling that Christ's devotion extended to dying for it (5:25) and that his love makes him assimilate the Church into the own body; "Men ought to love their wives as [being] their own bodies. He that loveth his wife, loveth himself. For no man ever hateth his own flesh, but nourisheth and cherisheth it, as also Christ does the Church: because we are members of his body. For this cause shall a man leave his father and mother, and shall cleave to his wife, and they shall be two in one flesh. This is a great mystery, but I say it relates to Christ and the Church." (5:28-32.)

A man's love for his wife springs from the fusion of two beings into a single body. Husbands should give full vent to this natural tendency, for such love is a holy thing, and though born out of a union of the flesh, its model is the highest heavenly one, Christ himself. Just as the identification of the Church with his own body makes Christ love his spouse, so does the identification of the wife with the husband's body give him a duty to love her. Everything points to the analogy between the duties resulting from the mystical union and the carnal union being founded on an identification of two beings in one flesh. Mystical union calls to mind the Genesis text "They shall be two in one flesh" as much as does the union between man and wife.

When we discourse about the union of Christ and the Church we take the union of man and wife as a starting-point. St Paul does the reverse: the reality of the union of the faithful with the body of Christ, and the moral relationships resulting from it, help him to show how real are the union of marriage and the duties it brings. The union of Christ and his Church is much deeper than the union of marriage, and the identification in a single body more absolute. Union in the flesh is only a reflection and a sign, an earthly shadow, cast back over the beginnings of mankind, of the final and heavenly reality. The promise of Genesis—"They two shall be in one flesh"—is understood in a divine sense: Christ and the Church are wedded together for ever, and are united in a single body. "The body of Christ is the bridal chamber of the Church." (St Ambrose.)

The Christian community has one rite which both manifests and effects its union with Christ in a single body, the Eucharist: "The chalice of benediction which we bless, is it not the communion of the blood of Christ? And the bread which we break, is it not the communion of the body of the Lord?" (1 Cor 10:16.) "Communion of the body and blood"—a phrase rich in meaning; it indicates participation in the body and blood, communion in Christ through his body and blood; there is added the unspoken idea that in that body and blood there is a community among ourselves; the presence of the next verse, which seems added over and above the central development, becomes clear only if we give the thought this nuance: "Because the bread is one, we in our multitude are but one body, because we all partake of this single bread." (Verse 17.) We are but one body, because we all eat the bread which is the one body of Christ and enter in communion with it. "One can see no reason why the Church should be named the body of Christ, and should in fact be so, except that by giving it his body, Christ transforms it into himself so that it may become his body and all may become his members." (St Albert the Great.)

This identifying of the Church with the individual body of Christ present in the Eucharist is simply St Paul's way of explaining the words of institution. He had "received" the eucharistic formula in this way: "This is my body which [is delivered] for you. This do for the commemoration of me . . . This chalice is the new testament in my blood. This do ye, as often as you shall drink, for the commemoration of me." (1 Cor 11:24f.) It is generally recognized that Paul is closer to the letter in reporting the words of consecration of the chalice than Matthew or Mark. Our Lord declares that the chalice, because of the blood it holds, constitutes the new testament.

The biblical use of *diatheke* (testament) is different from its normal profane use. In the language of the time, the word was a juridical term meaning a testamentary disposition. St Paul uses it twice in this sense: once in Gal 3:15, and again in Heb 9:16f.; but in the latter case the surrounding verses use the word in its biblical sense. In the twenty-three other cases of the word being used in the Pauline epistles (including Hebrews), it does not mean a will, but, as in the Bible, a divine dispensation, a scheme of relationship between God and his people brought about because God so wills.

God had declared a new *diatheke*, a new economy (Rom 9:27; Is 59:21; Jer 31:31ff.) from which sin was to be excluded, in which the law was to be written on men's hearts. St Paul defines this "new dispensation" by the presence of the Spirit, and contrasts it with the economy of the letter. (2 Cor 3:6; Jer 31:31ff.) The Apostle is the minister of this new religious form, in the service of the spiritual dispensation. Hence he gives the "two Testaments" approximately the same sense as we do (Gal 4:24–6).

In the formula handed on by St Paul, Christ declares that the eucharistic chalice, because it holds his blood, constitutes the new *diatheke*. There is nothing to suggest the juridical interpretation of the term; the Last Supper has nothing in common with the making of a will. Besides, Christ does not say that the chalice is *his* testament, but the new testament, thus recalling Jer 31:31ff.; he is contrasting the "new testament" with the old dispensation, which was also sealed in blood. Christ's work was to introduce a new economy by his death. Though at this moment he joins Jeremiah in calling it a *diatheke*, he generally speaks of it as the "Kingdom of God". The two ideas are closely related; the Kingdom of God is established at the same moment as God's plan comes into force, and the new relationship between God and man is formed. For St Paul, the "new *diatheke*" means the Christian institution in its concrete reality (2 Cor 3:6); everything abstract that might be contained in the idea is stripped away when he identifies it with "that Jerusalem which is above ... which is the mother of us all". (Gal 4:26.)

While the first part of the eucharistic formula is merely a statement of the real presence of the immolated body, the second stresses the new economy that is introduced by that immolated humanity and only indirectly mentions the presence of the blood; this chalice is the new testament because of the blood it contains. We cannot explain this relationship between Christ's blood and the *diatheke* by saying that the shedding of his blood opened the Christian era. It is not a question of the shedding of the blood, but of the chalice and the blood which it contains; this chalice *is* the new testament. Given the concrete meaning of the *diatheke* in St Paul, the version of the eucharistic formula preserved by him is a most forceful expression of the ecclesiastical sense of the Eucharist. The body and blood of the immolated Christ are at the centre of the Church, and it is contained in them as in its principle.

What these texts teach us about the relation between the Church and the body of Christ is also suggested by others. There are statements in St Paul which can be explained by no other supposition. Thus when he writes, "As many of you as have been baptized in Christ, have put on Christ. There is neither Jew nor Greek . . . you are all one in Christ Jesus. And if you be Christ's, then are you the seed of Abraham, heirs according to the promise." (Gal

The Resurrection of Christ

3:27–9.) Those Gentiles who have come to believe have entered the race of Abraham, because they have put on Christ. This is a legitimate reasoning only if it be true that the Christian is united to the bodily humanity of his Saviour: inclusion in Christ only makes us descendants of Abraham if it unites us to Christ's bodily being, for that bodily being is the only link between him and the patriarch.

It is true that the Apostle seems to recognize a descent from Abraham by faith alone, unconnected with his flesh: "It is written: Abraham believed God, and it was reputed to him unto justice. Know ye therefore that they who are of faith, the same are of the children of Abraham." (Gal 3:6; cf. Rom 4:11.) If the Apostle's mind were entirely expressed in this text we should have cause for astonishment. That undoubtedly carnal seed of Abraham to whom the promises were given, would, by a somewhat arbitrary exegesis, be identified with all who copy Abraham in his faith.

But St Paul realizes that it was to Israel that the promises were made: "To whom belongeth the glory ... the testaments ... the promises." (Rom 9:4; 3:1f.) By making faith the sole heir of those promises, he means to exclude the Law. It is faith that makes us like Abraham in the act which won justification for him, not the Law (Rom 4:13ff.), for the faith of the Father of Israel was already reputed to him unto justice (Rom 4:10–12), before he carried out the essential act of the Law upon himself. It was still under the rule of faith that the promise was given to him, and no condition attached to its fulfilment but faith alone. (Rom 4:13-16.) Justice could, therefore, come to us, and sons, heirs of the promise, could be born to Abraham quite outside the framework of the Law; only faith was necessary.

But this still gives us no principle whereby we can reduce the title "descendant of Abraham" to a merely moral relationship. The dispute between faith and the Law resolves itself in the moral sphere; faith is not set against a physical relationship with the patriarch. The question whether it is necessary to belong to the messianic race to benefit from the promises is still unresolved.

For St Paul this belonging certainly demands a moral condition, but one built upon a physical basis. This was, after all, the case with the first members of the race. Abraham had more than one son, yet "In Isaac alone shall thy seed be called. That is to say, not they that are the children of the flesh, are the children of God; but they that are the children of the promise, are accounted for the seed." (Rom. 9:7-8.) There must be not only birth, but a divine choice too. This law, which was valid for Isaac, remains valid for his descendants: "For all are not Israelites that are of Israel." (Rom 9:6.) The Apostle distinguishes a sonship according to the flesh, and a sonship according to the promise, and he anticipates the reality of the New Testament by calling this latter sonship according to the Spirit. (Gal 4:22ff.) Thus one can discern in the true descendant of Abraham a twofold parentage—the racial relationship, what is given by the flesh, and what is given from above, the promise or vocation to which man responds by faith.

Does it follow that when Abraham's seed multiply in Christ, one of these two links is broken? Are we left with only that faith which places us in the line of Abraham by likeness of soul but does not actually make us his sons? If so, the promise made to Abraham grows poorer as it grows wider. Though the beneficiaries of the promise are multiplying, Abraham would recognize them not as his seed but simply as his imitators. This would not seem to be St Paul's notion.

He has spiritualized the concept of the seed of Abraham, by applying it to the Church rather than to the race of old, but he has not impoverished it. This Jew who had grown up in the knowledge of messianic promises bound up with the race of Abraham did not conceive of there being a people of God without Abraham for their true father. In Rom 4, his faith seems to make the believer no more than an imitator of the patriarch, for that is the reasoning demanded by the context; but in fact, for St Paul, faith produces not merely assent of the mind, but a total adherence which transforms the believer into Christ. In Romans, the complexity of his thought is simplified; he stresses only faith, and a faith which seems to be merely an assent. But in Galatians (3:26-8), he synthesizes his whole doctrine: "You are all the children of God by faith, in Christ Jesus. For as many of you as have been baptized in

Christ, have put on Christ. There is neither Jew nor Greek . . . You are all one in Christ Jesus." By the faith expressed in baptism, the believer has clothed himself in the dead and risen Christ, and is therefore, even in his body, lifted up to a kind of life in which all the differences resulting from carnal bodiliness are done away with; he takes his place in a new race, the race of Christ, in his spiritual body. "And if you be Christ's, then are you the seed of Abraham, heirs according to the promise." (Gal 3:29.) Even more than was the birth of Isaac, this birth in Christ is wholly according to the Spirit. And it is at the same time a birth into Abraham, for it is the effect of being joined to and identified with the physical being of Christ, which was received from Abraham. The patriarch becomes the father of all who believe; he brings forth children in Christ, not now by generation according to the flesh, but through faith; we are his children in the body of Christ.

The consistency with which the body of Christ is put at the foundation of the messianic edifice is a striking manifestation of the doctrinal unity of the New Testament. The rejected stone becoming the head of the corner, the body rebuilt as the new Temple, the eating of the lamb becoming, in its fulfilment, the messianic banquet: all these images link the Church with the body of its Saviour, and some of them suggest the two as identified. St Paul's differs only in laying aside the language of figure, to unite the two literally.

vi. Summing-up

Let us remember that the new people is made up of all those who are joined to the body of Christ by the Spirit and by faith. God does things with greater reality than we would dare to believe. In his Son, who became one with our sinful race by being born in fallen flesh, he reunites us all, saves us and divinizes us, by making us to be reborn in that body in which sin was killed, in which all principles of division were destroyed, and in which the holiness of the Spirit blazes forth.

The Church had to wait for Easter to be born. The body of Christ is, as it were, its native soil, the root of its existence: it contains the Church and gives it life. But that body is the one that was immolated and glorified: the stone taken up again with honour, the paschal lamb, the Temple rebuilt in three days.

Before his exaltation, Christ in his physical nature was no more than a living being, a living soul, like his father Adam. (1 Cor 15:45.) To transform our flesh into himself, he had accepted a humanity descended from Adam, made up of the weight of the flesh, and an animating principle to match, the soul. This soul, and the compound being it animated, formed a living reality, but one which could not communicate life outside itself. St Paul makes this quite clear in the contrast he makes between the two Adams (1 Cor 15:45.) The limits of the soul's power of life are the limits of the one body it informs. The physical life of Adam does not overflow to other beings, nor contain them in itself.

Theologians Today: F. X. Durrwell

As with his life, so with his radius of action, natural man is circumscribed by the limits of the flesh. His action cannot, of itself, work at a distance; it can only affect the surroundings with which it actually comes into contact. And the contact of the flesh has no power to save. Christ declared, "It is the Spirit that quickeneth: the flesh profiteth nothing." (Jn 6:64.) He had just been teaching that his flesh was to give life to the world. But he was not speaking of the flesh in its natural state, to be assimilated by digestion. Such flesh, thus eaten, would profit nothing towards eternal life.

It did not matter that Christ's bodily humanity, in its carnal phase, could not communicate its life to us, for every man already had that life by birth.

In his death and resurrection, Christ was changed from a living soul into a life-giving Spirit. The physical Christ became spirit, even his material nature being divinized. He was no longer a "flesh that profiteth nothing", but a "spirit that quickeneth". The spirit is an overflowing principle, a soul wide open, endowed with limitless power, with a universal power of giving life. Matter, which limits and divides, which is weak, henceforward borrows the qualities of spirit; it loses its narrowness and lays aside its weakness. Christ in his bodily humanity becomes capable of giving life to the world, and containing it within himself. He does not multiply himself in the ordinary way of nature, lighting new fires of life from his own; he becomes many while remaining one. The very life of this human nature

The Resurrection of Christ

communicates itself, or rather, Christ communicates himself, assimilating us to him in the life of his bodily humanity, and clothing us in his being (Gal 3:27), in such a way as to make us into his body, into his actual bodily human nature.

It is a life filled with mystery, of which the only possible principle can be the Spirit of God who baffles all our experience. No bodily life lived according to the flesh could claim such power.

Since the Church is the body of Christ, in whom the Saviour lives the life of his embodied glory, it was necessary that its birth should await Easter. But on that day it was born, at the same moment as the glorified body with which it is identified, but to which it adds nothing. We may say that the body of Christ rose as a mystical body.

2. The Sacrament of Scripture

"In the sacred books the Father who is in Heaven meets his children with great love and speaks with them; and the force and power in the word of God is so great that it remains the support and energy of the Church, the strength of faith for its sons, the food of the soul, the pure abiding source of spiritual life."—*Dogmatic Constitution on Divine Revelation*, VI, 21.

The sacraments exist to make contact between men and the Word of God at the point when that Word is pronounced for our salvation: in the man Jesus and in his action redeeming us. Their name, "sacraments", means "mysteries", because by them the mystery of "the redemption that is in Christ Jesus" is accessible to mankind.

Holy Scripture, too, is a kind of sacrament—not one of the seven, of course, yet comparable to them because intended like them to link us with the word of salvation in the redeeming Christ. That once-spoken word came from the Father, and with it have come many words to us, like circles spreading out from the Word falling into the sea of mankind, all round it in time, spreading to the beginnings of centuries and the ends; or the echoing and re-echoing of the Word spoken in the redeeming Incarnation. These words are at work for God's designs of which Christ is the fullness; they are intended to lead men to the centre from which they grow and which by growing they extend—to the mystery of salvation which is in Christ. One may say that Scripture is also, in its own way, a sacrament to incorporate us into the redeeming Christ.

1. Holy Scripture, the Presence of the Redeeming Christ

rom patristic times, theology has related the two mysteries of Scripture and the Incarnation. There exists a real analogy between them. As Bossuet said: "He [the Word] took a kind of second body, I mean, the word of his Gospel". Through the action of the Holy Ghost in the Virgin Mary, God's own thought —his Word—was clothed in human nature, with its imperfections, and dwelt amongst us. Through another action of the Holy Ghost, in the sacred writers, in the womb of their intellect, God's thought was introduced into humanity, taking the form of human thought, and dwelt amongst us.

This divine thought, conceived from all eternity, eternally, one, holy and infinite, God has conceived in time, in the imperfection of the things of time, fragmentary, complex and limited. He has conceived it through the minds of men, which are limited both in themselves and by the restrictions of the time and place in which they function. The Word has put off its glory, taken the form of a servant, and come to dwell amongst us.

In the office for the Blessed Sacrament, the Church sings its happiness at possessing the incarnate Word in its midst in the Eucharist: "Neither is there nor has there been any other nation so great, that hath gods so nigh them, as our God is present to all our

The Sacrament of Scripture

petitions". The words are taken from Deuteronomy (4:7), and were used by the Jews to express the pride they felt in having a God who spoke to them, and whose thought and will for them they possessed in the sacred scrolls they carried with them. "For what other nation is there so renowned that hath ceremonies, and just judgements, and all the law, which I will set forth this day before your eyes?" (4:8). This praise which we now sing of the Incarnation and the Eucharist was first uttered to glorify Scripture, which was a sort of first incarnation of God's thought.

Having sung at length the divine origins of Wisdom and its eternal prerogatives, "I came out of the mouth of the Most High . . . From the beginning, and before the world, I was created . . .", Ecclesiasticus concludes: "All these things are the book of life and the [book of the] covenant of the Most High . . . who filleth up wisdom as the waters of Phison, and as the Tigris in the days of the new fruits." (24:5, 14, 32, 35.) In Scripture God's wisdom is already incarnate, flowing in the sacred book like a river between its banks. Israel made that divine presence on object of worship. The tables of the Law were placed in the Ark; in the synagogues, the Bible, contained in a cupboard facing the people, was the only object of worship. No one touched it till he had washed his hands, and then with much reverence.

Similarly, there is an intense presence of God in the books of the New Testament, but closer and more evident. Before becoming human in the thoughts and words of men, God's wisdom, which wrote the New Testament, took human flesh, and it is that incarnate Wisdom, Christ in his glory, who dwells amongst us in the books of the New Testament. For it is he who is the author of the New Testament. "The members [the Apostles] wrote what the Head inspired them to. Christ dictated to them, as to his hands, which of his words and actions he wanted us to know about." (St Augustine.)

One text in St John shows us that the opened side of Christ in glory is the source whence the books of the New Testament flow:

> If any man thirst, let him come to me, and let him that believeth in me drink. As the Scripture saith: *Out of his belly shall flow rivers of living water.*

From Christ's belly the rivers will flow—we should translate this Hebrew phrase by saying they will flow from Christ's heart. And "this he said of the Spirit which they should receive who believed in him"; he said it of the Holy Spirit whose tremendous outpouring in the last days had been spoken of by the Prophets. From Christ's sacred body where the soldier's lance struck him, as from the rock of Sinai, would flow the rivers of the New Testament, all the graces of the Kingdom, and also those of Scripture— the graces by which Scripture would be inspired, by which it would be read and understood, by which it would give life to the world. All these rivers will flow from that open side on the day of his redeeming

The Sacrament of Scripture

glory. Until that day, "the Spirit was not given, because Jesus was not yet glorified". (Jn 7:39.) "O heart of my beloved", cried St John Eudes, "I adore you as the source of all the holy words in this book." The Evangelists came, and each drank from that spring. "He drank the rivers of the gospel from the sacred fount of the Lord's heart", we say of the Apostle John in the office for his feast.

The New Testament is not Christ's book because it tells his story; it is his book because it is from him, born out of the wound in his heart, born like a child. Every word of Scripture is a grace of the Spirit of Jesus, a thought of everlasting life which flowed from his heart along with his blood: "And there came out blood and water", the water of the Spirit with the blood of immolation. With their sure instincts, the saints felt this redeeming presence in the New Testament. St Ignatius of Antioch wrote: "I take refuge in the Gospel as in the flesh of Jesus Christ." Other saints were to love to hide in Christ's heart, but St Ignatius sought his refuge in the Gospel, in the revelation of the Christian mystery, for that gospel was like a sacrament of the redeeming Christ, like a field in which, as St Jerome said, the treasure was hidden, the treasure of Christ himself.

In Christian worship Holy Scripture is forever linked with that supreme sacrament of Christ's body and the redemption, the Eucharist; the same name is used for both: "This chalice", Our Lord said, "is the New Testament"; this book also we call the New Testament; chalice and book, each in its own way, contain the New Covenant, the mystery of our redemption in Christ. The analogy is tremendous: "I think myself that Christ's body is [also] his gospel", says St Jerome, "the bread of Christ and his flesh is the divine word and heavenly doctrine." The early Church, struck by the resemblance between these two sacraments of Christ's presence, placed together, as on "two tables"—as the *Imitation of Christ* puts it—side by side, the Bread of Christ and the Book, invited the faithful to sit equally at both, to feed upon their Saviour and upon the salvation that was in him.

2. *Communion in Christ through Sacred Scripture*

For, in every form, Christ's presence among men has that same purpose. By his very being and in every thing he does, Christ is always the Redeemer; his presence is there to create a communion of salvation with men. This Scripture does; it, too, establishes a communion, different from the Eucharist but real none the less, a communion of thought between two people who love each other and talk together, one of whom is Christ.

Whenever we read his Scriptures with faith, Christ speaks. It was long ago that he inspired his Apostles, and centuries have passed since. But though the human writing of the Book was something that happened in the past, the inspired words still live in the moment when they are spoken by Christ. "This was written for us, and preserved for us; it is recited for us and will also be recited for our descendants,

The Sacrament of Scripture

right up to the end of time." (St Augustine.) The redeeming action of Christ in glory knows no succession of time; he speaks to the heart of the Church in eternity. The thoughts formulated by the Apostles and put into writing at a given moment of history are addressed to the Church of all the ages in an eternal present. Men are coming into existence now, are now reading Christ's word with faith, are hearing Christ speaking to them now.

Because Scripture is an everlasting word, always being said, the epistle to the Hebrews introduces all its quotations from Scripture by saying, "The Holy Ghost saith", "The Holy Ghost doth testify" (Heb 3:7; 10:15)—all in the present tense.

Christ speaks to us at this moment, but not like a friend far away communicating by letter; "God is not far from every one of us" (Acts 17:27) and "Christ dwells in our hearts." (Eph 3:17.) We sit at his feet and listen to him: "We must listen to the Gospel as to Christ amongst us", "the Gospel is the very mouth of Christ", a sacrament of his words to us. (St Augustine.) There is no human intermediary between his word and our mind; the sound we hear is actually his voice. According to St Thomas, God has two far from equal ways of teaching us: he speaks through an intermediary in human books of religious instruction, but "he speaks directly to our minds in sacred Scripture". (St Augustine.) Tired of hearing only a distant echo of Christ's voice from human lips, saints like St Thérèse of Lisieux resolved to read nothing but Scripture.

Theologians Today: F. X. Durrwell

This communion with Christ in thought is even closer than that between two people speaking together. When we look for the truth hidden in the text of Scripture, Christ can communicate the meaning of his words directly to our minds. I can read a given human book, and learn a philosophical truth from it. But what I get from its words depends on my perspicacity; I understand it only in proportion to my intelligence. The author may be dead, but even were he alive, he could not communicate to his reader the same understanding of the truth he is expressing that he has himself. The writer's thought comes to me not directly, but through signs, through words which I must interpret. But when we hear the words of Scripture, "the Master is in our hearts" (St Augustine) and communicates the same understanding of the truths they express that he himself has; he arouses in us his own sentiments: "Let the word of Christ dwell in our hearts in all its riches." (Col 3:16.) It is a wonderful communion of mind and heart—the communion of Mary of Bethany, of the disciples on the road to Emmaus.

This communion, too, is effective, giving eternal life. Of Scripture as of the Eucharist it can be said, "Pinguis est panis"—it is a substantial bread. For Christ lives now only in his redemptive act, given to God for mankind, immortal in his death for them, and forever an instrument of God's action in raising up to eternal life. Every presence and every action of Christ works redemption. When he appeared in the

The Sacrament of Scripture

evening of Easter Day, he sent the Apostles out to forgive sins. In the same way he made them write the pages of the New Testament for the remission of sins and the salvation of men.

By we know not what hidden influence, Scripture bestows a spirit of life on those who read it with faith. "Was our heart not burning within us, whilst he spoke?" (Lk 24:32); "The word of God is living and effectual" (Heb 4:12), it is the "sword of the spirit" (Eph 6:17). If ordinary human words, noble or degraded, can transform a man by their psychological dynamism, how much more must the word of God penetrate and pierce to the very depths of the soul, for it is "more piercing than any two-edged sword; and reaching unto the division of the soul and the spirit, of the joints also and the marrow". (Heb 4:12.)

It is not merely that God's word contains the thoughts of Christ, lofty and profound, which can stir up man's heart; but it is spoken for *me* and for *my* salvation; it is spoken by my saviour, in the grace of the Holy Spirit who flows from his pierced side. The Gospel is a message of redemption, a sacrament of salvation, in which "the Holy Ghost works in efficacious words". (Paschasius Radbert.)

"Attend unto reading." (1 Tim 4:13.) For "the holy scriptures can instruct thee to salvation, by the faith which is in Christ Jesus. All scripture, inspired of God, is profitable to each, to reprove, to correct, to instruct in justice, that the man of God may be perfect, furnished to every good work". (2 Tim 3:15–17.)

Theologians Today: F. X. Durrwell

Scripture is the treasure of "the man of God"; it is that rich treasure from which the householder "bringeth forth new things and old" (Mt 13:52) to accomplish "every good work". That good work is first of all accomplished actually in the heart of the man of God; the word is planted there, grows there and bears fruit there ("the word of truth . . . bringeth forth fruit and groweth" (Col 1:5–6)); it gives consolation there, too, that joy which glows where there is salvation, whereby we are born to the hope of the Last Day: "For what things soever were written were written for our learning: that through patience and the comfort of the Scriptures, we might have hope." (Rom 15:4.)

The Fathers seem to have been unable to find images strong enough to describe the banquet of redemption offered on the table of Scripture. The Gospel, according to St Jerome, is true food and true drink; Scripture is an ocean of fullness, says St Ambrose, a cup from which we drink Christ, a cup that is a river whose waves delight the city of God. It is the cure for all our ills, says St Augustine: "Take and drink; all sickness of soul finds its remedy in Scripture." The Eucharist, says St John Chrysostom, makes us as fierce lions in face of the devil. Also, says St Athanasius, Scripture puts our adversary to flight, for "in Scripture the Lord is present, and the demons, who cannot bear his presence, cry: I beg you, do not torment us before our time. They burn simply from seeing the Lord present".

Thus the banquet of Scripture feeds and

The Sacrament of Scripture

strengthens just as does the eucharistic banquet of Christ's immolated flesh; and like it, it has its joys, "the chaste delights of Scripture" spoken of by St Augustine, "the comfort of the Scriptures" which gives us hope (Rom 15:4), that great comfort which made the Maccabees say, "We needed none of these things, nor any one, having for our comfort the holy books that are in our hands". (1 Macc 12:9.)

Scripture and the Eucharist are the life-force and the joy of the Church, because they are for her a communion in the body given and blood shed for us. Other than that banquet there exists only what this life can offer us: "We have in this world only this one good thing: to feed upon his flesh and drink his blood, not only in the [eucharistic] sacrament, but in the reading of Scripture". (St Jerome.)

Despite its own efficaciousness, Scripture does not enter into any kind of competition in our souls with that other sacrament of presence and communion, the Eucharist; it does not supplant it, or make it unnecessary. The central point of Christian worship is the incarnate Word in his eternal sacrifice. Scripture comes to us from that centre, and must canalize our minds and hearts towards it. It is by the Eucharist that Christ is present to us in the reality of his body, in the reality of his immolation and his glory. So Scripture must collaborate with the sacrament to unite believers with the redeeming Christ.

In the Mass, the splendour of Scripture comes to surround the sacred body of Christ on all sides, as the royal purple of the incarnate Word in his immolation, as the veil of the Holy of Holies in which the eternal sacrifice is offered—a veil which is not there to hide but to reveal the way into the sanctuary. It was in this way, through the veil of the Scriptures, that the world of the Old Testament was brought to Christ.

Many non-Catholic Christians read Scripture more assiduously than many Catholics, but do not feed on the Eucharist. Among a lot of them there is a profound tendency not to accept the incarnation of the Word in its ultimate reality, but to prefer what seems to be a worship of God's transcendence—to prefer, at least in practice, the spoken Word to the personal Word, to remain in the Old Testament, on the threshold of the fullness of the Incarnation. Many Catholics have a tremendous devotion to the Eucharist, but neglect Scripture. Many of them, perhaps, do not therefore know the personal Word as well as they might, and are not in the best possible dispositions to receive him in the Eucharist. For the secret of opening one's heart to that one Word is contained most fully in Scripture.

3. *Necessary Dispositions for a Fruitful Reading of Scripture*

God allows us to "taste his good word" (Heb 6:5), but we do not always appreciate its savour. This bread is no more acceptable every day to all tastes than was the manna in the desert, than is the Eucharist. Our soul must be disposed to receive God's word.

The Sacrament of Scripture

To read in faith. We must have ears to hear the Word of God which are not the ears of the body: "Let him that hath ears, hear what the Spirit saith to the churches." (Rev 2:7). The ears to hear are the ears of faith. It is faith which opens the word of God to us. "The word of God worketh in you who have believed.' (1 Thess 2:13.)

Like every heavenly reality offered to us during our life on earth, Scripture has two facets—one accessible to the senses, the other visible to faith alone. It was so with Christ, whom his enemies saw with their eyes and nailed to the Cross, but whom his believers adored. It is thus with the Church, whose human face can be seen by all, but whose mystery is hidden for many. It is thus also with the Eucharist which to some is simply bread, and to others the body of the glorified Christ.

There are various ways of approaching Scripture, and not all of them lead to an encounter with Christ. Scholars without faith can make Scripture an object of investigation; but there is no critical apparatus that can bring them to the heart of Scripture, to the point of meeting with Christ. It has been said that Scripture is a locked house with the key inside. To enter it one must live in it, one must be in Christ, in his house which is the Church. One must be inside faith. This is yet one more sphere in which it is true that "whosoever hath, to him shall be given". (Lk 8:18.)

"My sheep hear my voice", said Our Lord (Jn 10:16.) Those outside may hear the words, but only the flock hear the voice, the voice which reveals the person. Thus it was on Easter morning that one of Christ's sheep recognized the Lord by the sound of his voice. There are the words, there is the voice; the first express ideas, the second a person. The words of Scripture can be compared with ordinary human words, but the voice is incomparable because the person it reveals is unique. While the believer listens to the succession of words, behind the closed doors of his soul he hears the voice, and the Word reveals himself. Only faith has ears to hear the voice; it alone establishes contact with Christ. When he hears the voice, and feels that contact with our Lord, the believer knows that the words are addressed to him. Each sheep is called by his name, the encounter is personal, and becomes a dialogue. "Mary", said Christ, and Mary answered, "Rabboni!"

By the light of faith Scripture is seen to have a dimension that no other book has. It is not invariably the finest of all literature. Not all its lines contain profound ideas, and even the most striking may have had their edges blunted by long use. One can hardly deny that there are human books superior to some parts of Scripture. But to the believer, these words offer a dimension of mystery, a stirring resonance: for it is the Lord who speaks them. One may recall how Mozart once played the clavichord in the house of a rich burgher of Prague. At the end his host, greatly impressed, said, "Would that I were the Emperor! I should give you a pat on the shoulder, and say, "You really have played well, Mozart!'

The Sacrament of Scripture

That would be enough for you. But who am I to be able to reward you?" Similarly, the word which of itself would be but a pebble on the roadway, is a diamond when spoken by the Lord.

To read in the light of Easter. The Christ whose voice Scripture makes us hear is the Lord of Easter, the Christ of faith. He became the author of that book in the light and fire of the glory of his raising by the Father. The rivers of the Spirit, of all the charismata of the New Testament, the gift of scriptural inspiration, all flow from his pierced side after his return to his Father. The Apostles and Evangelists understood this, and wrote "in that day", in the light of Easter. Even Christ's life on earth was told from the point of view of his resurrection, in faith in the glorified Christ. The thought of his death and resurrection is the golden thread which binds together the separate pages of the Gospel and makes it a book.

Again, it was the risen Christ, source of the Spirit, who opened the minds of his disciples on the road to Emmaus, and interpreted the Scriptures to them.

Just as Magdalen could no longer catch hold of the glorified Lord with her bodily hands, so scholars cannot hear him with their human minds. He is accessible only to faith. He can only be seen, touched and heard by his disciples, those who eat and drink with him after the Resurrection. (Acts 10:41.)

To him who believes, our Lord's face appears even in the pages of the Old Testament. It is Christ, dead and risen again, who gives the whole Bible its unity and meaning. If it is divorced from the glorified Christ it is a dead letter, a story written in sand, a set of laws which cannot give life. "The letter killeth, but the spirit quickeneth." (2 Cor 3:6.) "The letter" here is the realities of the Old Testament considered in themselves, and all the things of this world. "The spirit" means reality in its fullness, the reality of heaven, of which all other realities are but fleeting shadows. The reality of heaven comes at the end, according to the promise given in the Old Testament; it is none other than the very Spirit of God, in whom all will be consummated, all be made one and living.

Now the risen Christ "is the Spirit". (2 Cor 3:17.) He is the solid body whose shadow was cast right back to the beginning of the world. (Col 2:17.) The reality of all things is in him, and without him all is shadow and death. In him all becomes spirit and life. For he has been "enlivened in the Spirit" (1 Pet 3:18), in the total outpouring of the Holy Ghost. He has been so completely transformed in the Spirit, that he himself has become a "quickening spirit" (1 Cor 15:45), and that we may speak of the body of the glorified Christ as in a sense the body of the Holy Ghost. In his redeeming glory, he has become the centre of creation. (Col 1:16.) "And I, if I be lifted up, will draw all things to myself" (Jn 12:32); he draws to himself not only all men, but all things, making himself the centre of nature and history, of the Old Testament and the New, lord of the past and the future; Elijah and Moses, prophecy and the Law, the whole of the Old Covenant, all turn their faces towards the transfigured Christ. He is God's "Amen" (2 Cor 1:20) to the promise of the Old Testament, and to all the promises contained in the first creation, "because in him it hath well pleased the Father that all the fullness [of the universe] should dwell". (Col 1:19.)

The unbeliever looking at the Bible sees only the dead letter, the disparate elements; his eyes are bound. The believer reads with uncovered eyes, and has only to open the Old Testament to find himself face to face with our Lord in glory; he feels himself "transformed into the same image from glory to glory, as by the action of the Lord who is the Spirit". (2 Cor 3:14-18.)

A simple and living faith. The believer opens the sacred book with respect, just as in the synagogue at Nazareth, Christ stood up to read the prophecy of Isaiah (Lk 4:16), filled with veneration for the Word of his God and Father. Faith reads with a simple and sincere heart. "How should one read the sacred Scriptures?", someone asked Padre Nadal, one of the first Jesuits. "Like a good old grandmother", he replied. Timothy had read Scripture at the knees of his grandmother and his mother, with these women's faith: "I call to mind that faith which is in thee, which also dwelt first in thy grandmother Lois and in thy mother Eunice. . . . From thy infancy thou hast known the holy scriptures, which can instruct thee to salvation, by the faith which is in Christ Jesus." (2 Tim 1:5; 3:15.)

It is an obedient faith: "And they shall all be taught of God" (Jn 6:45), God's pupils, desiring to "do truth" (Jn 3:21). We must read Scripture with the hope of finding there our marching orders: "Good master, what shall I do that I may receive life everlasting?" (Mk 10:17). For it is Christ's essence to redeem, and no-one enters into communion with him unless he wants to be saved by him. The Fathers used to say that Scripture was a letter sent by God from his kingdom far away, to draw us to him.

A loving faith. A letter from God must be read with loving faith. Kierkegaard said people should read the Bible not so much as critics and scholars, but "before God", as a man would read a letter from his fiancée. For to understand one must love. St Paul asks that the eyes of our heart be enlightened. (Eph 1:18.) It is the heart that sees, it is love that knows; in the biblical sense of the word, knowledge is mutual possession: "Blessed are they who know by the delight they have experienced, with what gentleness, what allurement, the Lord deigns to explain the Scriptures to us in prayer and meditation... He does it when he lights up our hearts with the beams of charity". (St Bernard.)

To read prayerfully. If Christ is to come and eat with his own, he must find in them "a large dining-room furnished". (Mk 14:15.) It is the work of prayer to

The Sacrament of Scripture

prepare hearts for his coming, by the longing it expresses. Every parousia of Christ comes as an answer to longing: "Come, Lord Jesus!"

"In truth", said St Augustine to the *studiosi venerabilium litterarum*, "to understand Scripture, what is essential is to pray." He gave an example of this himself:

> Let your Scripture be my chaste delight . . . Give me freely the time I need to meditate on the secrets of your law; close not to them that knock. It was not for nothing that you willed so many mysterious pages written. Have not these forests too their stags who take refuge and comfort there, come and go in them, feed, sleep and ruminate there?—O Lord, perfect your work in me! Reveal those pages to me! Behold, your word is my joy; indeed your word is a joy higher than all pleasures."

In a letter to Gregory the Wonderworker, his "most dear lord", Origen wrote:

> Well then, my son and lord, give yourself above all to the study of Holy Scripture, but you must give yourself. It requires great attention to read of the things of God, to say or think nothing unfitting.
>
> And, giving yourself to read the things of God with the dispositions of faith pleasing to him, knock that the things contained in them may be opened, that that door may be opened of which Christ said, "The doorkeeper will open to him". Giving yourself to that reading, seek with sincerity

and with an unshakeable faith in God what is hidden from so many: the meaning of the sacred books.

Do not be content with seeking and knocking, for it is prayer above all that is needed for the understanding of the things of God. Our Lord urges us to it, saying not only, "Knock and it shall be opened; seek and you shall find", but also, "Ask and you shall receive".

It is my paternal love, that I dare say this to you.

We address that prayer to Christ, whose heart is the source of all the words in Scripture. We address it to our Lady representing the whole of the believing Church for which the sacred books are written, that Church which weighs and compares together the words of God. Her own heart was the most fertile field in which the seed of redemption was sown. Of the Gospel of St John, Origen declares: "No one can understand it who has not leant on the breast of Christ and received Mary as his Mother".

The Scripture as the source of prayer. Prayer prepares a place for the Lord in the reader, makes ready for an intimate communion. But reading Scripture, in its turn, rouses a desire for his coming and invites to prayer. "Sacred Scripture is a calling towards our heavenly home, it transports the reader from the desires of this world to the love of higher things. The more one meditates upon it the more one loves it." (St Gregory the Great.)

The Sacrament of Scripture

Every sacrament of the Church is a pasch celebrated with Christ, and a parasceve (preparation for the Pasch), an actual parousia (presence) and a preparation for the Coming. Thus the Eucharist is now the true banquet of the end of time, the pasch in the Kingdom, and it is also still the manna of the Exodus, which supports and helps us on in our journey to the Promised Land. So it is with the mystery of Scripture. Christ comes and talks to the faithful, but only in the inn at Emmaus, in the half-light of the upper room, under the veil of the letter. He celebrates the pasch in darkness. But the night is past midnight, the dim light of the coming day (Rom 13:12) fills the Church with longing and hope. The faithful bear within them the word of God "as a light that shineth in a dark place, until the day dawn, and the day star arise in your hearts" (2 Pet 1:19), ". . . the root and stock of David, the bright and morning star". (Rev 22:16.) In this world every communion in the pasch is a mystery of hope as well as a beginning of possession, a banquet which satisfies yet gives rise to hunger. As she folds up the letter her Saviour has sent, the betrothed girl sighs, "Come, Lord Jesus!" It is upon this longing that Scripture finishes on the last page of the Book of Revelation (22:20), upon this that our reading of Scripture concludes.

3. The Mass in our Lives

"At the Last Supper, our Saviour instituted the eucharistic sacrifice of his Body and Blood. He did this in order to perpetuate the sacrifice of the Cross throughout the centuries until he should come again, and so to entrust to his beloved Spouse, the Church, a memorial of his death and resurrection: a sacrament of love, a sign of unity, a bond of charity, a paschal banquet in which Christ is consumed, the mind is filled with grace, and a pledge of future glory is given to us."—*Constitution on the Sacred Liturgy*, II, 47.

Only one man was able to pass from this world of sin and death into the eternal life of God. None before him and none since. From sin to salvation, from death to life, there is no bridge for any but that one man: Christ. He alone could effect human redemption. He did it in his own person, in his death and glorification.

If any other man is to be saved, is to pass in his turn from this world to God, he must participate in that one great act in which salvation lies. In his death and resurrection, Christ is the bridge and the passage. The man whom he wills to save, he must first place upon that bridge; he must literally take him into his own redemptive humanity, must make him share in his own passage, in his own death in which he is glorified.

But how can I be united to Christ in his redeeming act? He died far away two thousand years ago; how can I join him in that one redeeming act? Were I to go to Palestine, I should not find him now. I might kiss the ground where Christ's blood was shed, but I still should not find him. I cannot become contemporary with his death and resurrection. And even had I been contemporary with Christ, even had I been present at his agony upon Calvary, I could not have attached myself to his redeeming pasch, which bore him from this world to the Father. For his pasch was personal to him. Redemption was simply his own death. And one man's death cannot be another's.

There is no redemption except in Christ and for him.

1. *The Meaning of the Mass*

Before he celebrated his own pasch, Christ created a mysterious means of sharing in his death and resurrection—a paschal sacrament that could introduce men into his redeeming act. He took bread into his holy hands and said: "Take ye and eat; this is my body given for you". The Eucharist is Christ's body in the act of redemption, in that unique and personal act which happened once and for all in history, under Pontius Pilate, at the gates of Jerusalem, but which comes mysteriously into our time and place so as to become ours.

The Mass makes present Christ's body and his redeeming act. The Redemption is in Christ, personal to him, as it were takes substance in him. For it to be communicated to us, Christ must in some way enter our substance; our personality must be laid open to his. The Mass is our Saviour himself communicating himself to us: "Take ye and eat; this is my body". This food is not Christ's body as it might have been

The Mass in our Lives

at any moment of his life on earth, but Christ's body in the act of redeeming us. When Christ asks us to this meal, he says, "Take and eat, this is my body given for you". He does not simply say, "This is my body", but "my body given for you". The body of Christ is communicated to us as "given", as dead to this world and glorified in God. When he consecrates the chalice, Christ says: "This chalice is my blood [at this moment] shed". (Cf. Lk 22:20.).

In the eucharistic discourse he promises: "The bread that I will give is my flesh [given] for the life of the world." (Jn 6:52.) St Paul reminds the Corinthians: "As often as you shall eat this bread, and drink the chalice, you shall show the death of the Lord." (1 Cor 11:26.) That death which St Paul speaks of and Christ speaks of, is Christ's death, the one and only death, *sub Pontio Pilato*. The Mass is Christ present in his one and only redeeming act, the sacrifice of Calvary becoming a reality of our lives too.

"How can it be a sacrifice?" ask Protestants. There is only one sacrifice of Christ: "By his own blood he entered once into the holies, obtaining eternal redemption." (Heb 9:12.) "By one oblation he hath perfected forever them that he hath sanctified." (Heb 10:14.) That is one of the key ideas of the Epistle to the Hebrews: the sacrifices of the Old Testament had constantly to be renewed because they were always ineffective, incapable of "sanctifying" man, of immolating him to himself and bringing him into the life-giving holiness of God. Christ, on the other hand, has offered a single sacrifice, perfect and sufficient, the sacrifice of the end of time, which fulfils and crowns all mankind's longing for salvation and sacrificial actions. By his death, Christ entered once for all into the sanctuary of divine life, and takes with him all his followers.

The Protestants are therefore quite right in their dogged affirmation of the absolute uniqueness of Christ's sacrifice. There is but that one, which took place once and for all, never repeated, never repeatable. Yet the Church believes that the Mass is a sacrifice. It believes it because of Scripture, and because of its own uninterrupted and most ancient tradition, through which the Holy Ghost speaks, "for the Spirit is the truth". (1 Jn 5:6.) The Church is faced with two apparently contradictory truths: the fact that Calvary is unique, and the fact that the Eucharist is a sacrifice. Like the faithful spouse, it accepts, even before it can understand, the word of the Lord it loves. The Church believes it: there is no sacrifice but that of the Cross, and every mass is a sacrifice.

Of these two truths, the prime and essential one is the uniqueness of Christ's sacrifice; the Church must hold this in all strictness. The Mass cannot be another sacrifice, a reproduction or repetition, a second, third or hundredth sacrifice following the one offered under Pontius Pilate. If it is a sacrifice, it must be that one and only one, made two thousand years ago, never repeated, never repeatable, but mysteriously brought into our lifetime.

The Mass in our Lives

There are millions of hosts, but one body of Christ. There are millions of masses said, but only one sacrifice of Christ, offered on Calvary, which enters into our lives: "Just as everywhere it is only one body that is offered, and not many bodies, so there is but one sacrifice". (St Thomas Aquinas.) The millions of masses offered through the ages in all parts of the world, are Christ present in the midst of his Church, in the unique moment of his sacrifice on Calvary.

When the priest says the words of consecration, he pauses in wonder at this *mysterium fidei*. For it is doubly a mystery—the mystery of Christ's unfathomable sacrifice, and the mystery of that sacrifice made present to us. Between the sacrifice of Calvary and the sacrifice of the altar the only difference is in the way it is present. The Mass is the one and only Tree of the Cross planted in our midst that we may eat its fruits.

A *mysterium tremendum*, said the early Christians, a fearful mystery. They were right. Christ is present to us in the most majestic moment of history, the moment of his sacrifice in which the world of sin dies, and the world of the last days is created in God's love. We sing, "Holy, Holy, Holy!" not only to acclaim the Lord coming in glory, but to adore the Godhead entering our lives at that moment.

A fearful mystery of faith, but a mystery of joy too. It is what gives the Church her exultant joy and her hope; it is her one treasure. Christ at the moment of the Redemption is in her midst, and with him all the riches of that redemption. We need only the faith to believe.

. . . That the Church may become Christ's body and take part in his redeeming act. Why should Christ, with his redemptive act, make himself present in every time and place? In order that the Church may, in every time and place, take part in his redemptive act. For, in order to be saved, the Church must unite itself to its Saviour, must die together with him, and rise with him.

What good would Christ's death have done me if he had been content simply to die for me? No-one can die for me, die in my place. Sin is in me, in my body, in my whole being. I am a sinner by my nature. If I am to be saved from my condition of sin and death, the Saviour must take me into himself, must make me die in him to my life of sin and death, must transfer me into his holy and immortal risen life.

Thus our Saviour makes himself present in all times and places, here, this year, today, in order that I who live here today may today be caught up by him, may die to myself in Christ's own death, may be raised up by the divine action that raises Christ. That is Christ's purpose in placing himself, with his sacrifice, in our time and in our lives: to join the whole Church to his body, and turn her into his own sacrifice, that she may be Christ on earth in his redeeming sacrifice—one body in him, one death with him, and one resurrection.

The Mass is celebrated like a meal. We consume

The Mass in our Lives

the body of Christ in his death and glorification. This meal makes us Christ's body. "Because there is but one bread, we all form one body, all we who have partaken of that bread." (1 Cor 10:17.) We become Christ's body not simply in faith and charity, but literally. If we are to be saved, we must become Christ's body, for redemption is in that body and nowhere else. But the Mass is not just the presence of the Body and the meal of the Body; it is the presence of Christ in his sacrifice, and the meal is a participation in that sacrifice. Our Saviour takes us into himself and absorbs all our existence into his redeeming act.

Thus the Eucharist is a food which kills and brings to life, puts the man of this world to death and resurrects him into the life of God. Caught up in Christ's sacrifice, in his single sacrificial act, the Church of all ages, the Church throughout the world, becomes the very body of its Saviour in his redeeming act. The Church itself becomes Christ's sacrifice still present forever in the world until the parousia.

The Christ who redeems us, permanently risen, and by that resurrection fixed forever in death, is a heavenly reality, and cannot be present, in his own form, to the world he is going to save. He enters our sphere by means of the eucharistic sign, and makes the Church his own body present to the world, containing salvation for the world. Thus the Mass is celebrated in order that the Church may become the Mass, the one sacrifice of Christ still forever present on earth. In order that all Christians may become martyrs, either actual or virtual. In order that the whole world may become the Golgotha of Christ's death and resurrection, that the whole world may be saved. Until the parousia, the Church, through all its members who believe, hope and love, will be the redeeming Christ on earth, in his death and his risen life; it will be so in order that salvation may be accomplished in all men as it has been accomplished in Christ. Our Lord would not have instituted the Mass, he would not have needed to, if it were not for the purpose of making the unique redeeming sacrifice effective in us all.

2. *The Celebration of Mass*

Our eucharistic liturgy, then, must not be thought to consist simply in movements, in singing, signs and outward worship. To attain its goal, it must bring about, by those actions and signs, our participation in Christ and his act redeeming us.

We celebrate mass by dying and rising again in Christ. The liturgy would have no reality, indeed we should not be celebrating mass at all (either priests or people), if we did not participate in Christ in his death to "the world" and his life of glory. If we stop short at the gestures and hymns of a liturgy that is no more than a sign, then we are not exercising our Christian priesthood, we are not accomplishing in our own persons the sacrifice of Christ—for our salvation demands a real participation in the redeeming act.

The Mass in our Lives

Christ is a priest and an offerer of sacrifices by the death in which he is glorified. He did not celebrate a worship of sacramental signs; he did not offer a sacrifice external to himself. His priesthood brought with it no apparatus of ritual, no appearance of priesthood, no sacred gestures. Our Lord pontificated without altar, incense or candles. He did not bear a silk cross embroidered on a chasuble, but a wooden cross on which he was crucified. He intoned no ritual hymns; he said no liturgical prayers but the psalm phrases that expressed the intensity of his feelings, his longing for God and his help, and his complete abandonment to his Father: "I thirst" (Jn 19:28; Ps 69 (68):22); "My God, my God, why hast thou forsaken me?" (Mk 15:34; Ps 22(21):2); "Father, into thy hands I commend my spirit." (Lk 23:46; Ps 31(30):6.)

In Christ's sacrifice everything was reality—the gift of self, the immolation and the consecration. Everything was personal to Christ, inalienable and inseparable from him. His sacrifice was carried out in his own person, in his death to himself whereby he went to the Father. This reality of Christ's priesthood, the personal nature of his sacrifice, is another key theme of the Epistle to the Hebrews: ". . . neither by the blood of goats or of calves, but by his own blood, entered once into the holies." (Heb 9:12.) His sacrifice was nothing but the bloody, anguished gift of his own being, his own passage from the world to the Father. The veil through which he entered the Holy of Holies, the sanctuary of God, was not the thick canvas that the Jewish high priest lifted aside, but the destruction of his flesh, by which he opened a path to God (Heb 10:20.) This was the worship in spirit and in truth, the sacrifice of self in the charity of God.

Realizing this can hardly make us think the sacramental cult less important—Christ himself commanded, "Do this in commemoration of me": continue to celebrate this mysterious rite! But it can preserve it from any suggestion of routine, from any deviation from reality and truth. It removes the danger of any forgetting of essentials, of any return to a liturgy of shadows and figures. Christ died to abolish all merely external worship. When he died on the Cross, the veil of the Temple was rent; with Christ's death the Temple of this world's worship crumbled, never to be rebuilt. The only worship pleasing to God thenceforth was a personal worship, the worship personal to Christ. The Church has never known any priesthood apart from the priesthood inherent in the person of Christ; it has never admitted of any sacrifice but Calvary.

If the only Christian sacrifice is the death whereby Christ gave himself over to the glory of the Father, a death inseparably bound up with his own person— for Christ's death was to himself alone—who then can celebrate the Christian sacrifice? No-one but Christ. No-one, unless he be integrated into Christ and his sacrificial act, unless there be realized in him, by the mysterious power of God, the Lord's own pasch. To be real and of value to us, our liturgy demands that we be fitted into Christ, into his redeeming act. We should be no longer exercising the Christian priesthood, were we content to offer a sacrifice exterior to ourselves, a host held simply in our hands. How could we offer Christ's sacrifice if we merely celebrated his death with hymns of mourning, and his triumph with hymns of victory? Since Christ's sacrifice consists in Christ's dying and being glorified in God, we can offer it only by dying and rising in Christ.

One cannot therefore be a genuine celebrant of the Eucharist without a communion in Christ and a personal involvement in his redeeming mystery. Apart from that, the lay Christian can certainly perform the gestures of the Liturgy; the priest can even be the instrument whereby Christ makes himself present to his Church and offers himself in it. But if they are not personally associated in the redemptive act, in the love of Christ for his God, in his death to the world and in the grace of his resurrection, then the Mass will not be their sacrifice. They will be merely ministers of the sign, of what is imperfect and earthly in Christian worship; they will be like the priests of the Old Law, who offered a victim external to themselves. They will not be priests in spirit and in truth, not priests of a real and heavenly worship. They will not be offering the Christian sacrifice.

Such is the grandeur and magnificence of the Christian Liturgy: it can only be celebrated by those who celebrate it in Christ, those for whom their

Saviour's pasch becomes a personal reality. For since that time there has been but one Liturgy, containing the consummation of the world—the redeeming sacrifice of Christ.

All Christian life is a celebrating of the mystery of redemption. Thus the eucharistic celebration is inseparable from our lives. The liturgy of the sacraments is not an end in itself, but is ordered to the Church, and intended to make it become wholly Christ in his redeeming act. It is not the celebration of the sacraments which is the high point of the Church's activity; the Church is not primarily a community of worship—unless by worship one means that worship in spirit and truth which is a living participation in Christ's pasch—but a community of life and death in Christ.

That participation extends beyond the moment when the sacraments happen. St Paul did not speak of dying and rising with Christ only in baptism, but in his whole life: "I am crucified with Christ; I live now, not I, but Christ liveth in me." (Gal 2:19.) It is not just in the short time it takes to celebrate the Eucharist that the Church must be the Mass, the redeeming Christ present in the world, but throughout history till the parousia, for its own salvation and that of the world. Christ's liturgy on earth, solemn and unceasing, is none other than the very life of the Church.

The Church celebrates Christ's sacrifice even outside its liturgical action; the Church celebrates it in

The Mass in our Lives

its faithful who die to themselves through obedience, with Christ on the Cross; in those who struggle to gain heavenly love, who raise themselves out of this world towards purity and poverty of heart, with Christ who went to the Father; in all its faithful who work and suffer, who love God and neighbour, who give themselves for the salvation of others. In all of them the Church is the redeeming sacrifice, the Mass celebrated in spirit and in truth.

When a Christian, priest or layman, dies in faith and love, he is exercising his Christian priesthood for the last time, saying his last mass; he is playing his part, for the last time, in redeeming the world, and entering the fullness of Christ's death, the totality of his glory. That last mass will, by God's grace, be the holiest and most real of all. Not that our death can be more precious than the death of Christ we celebrate in the Eucharist, but because it is our most total sharing in it. Our liturgical celebrations, if they are to be real, must resemble that moment when we shall say, with Christ who accepts, adores and loves, "Father, into thy hands I commend my spirit".

The Mass is said in order that the whole Church and the whole of our life may become a mass, may become Christ's sacrifice always present on earth. St Francis de Sales resolved that he would spend the whole day preparing to say mass, so that whenever anyone asked what he was doing, he might always answer, "I am preparing for Mass". We also could resolve to make our whole lives a participation in the divine mystery of the Redemption, so that when anyone puts the question to us, we can always answer, "I am saying Mass".

4. Creation and the Apostolate

"He who is 'the image of the invisible God' (Col 1.15) is himself the perfect man. To the sons of Adam he restores the divine likeness which had been disfigured from the first sin on. Since human nature as he assumed it was not annulled, by that very fact it has been raised up to a divine dignity in our respect too. For by his incarnation the Son of God has united himself in some fashion with every man. He worked with human hands, he thought with a human mind, acted by human choice, and loved with a human heart."—*Pastoral Constitution on the Church in the Modern World*, I, 1, 22.

The relations between God and men could be conceived as different from what they are and the salvation effected by Christ understood in such a way that it would not constitute God's basic project. For some centuries now Christian thought has been dominated by a theology which, although centred on the death of Christ—but on this alone—did not place this death at the heart of human existence. It was a theology of sin and its expiation: it taught that the plan of redemption had come to renew God's creative plan, impaired by Adam's sin, or had been added on to the original plan. In his very depths, at his creation, therefore, man did not depend on the love of God as manifested in the redeeming Christ: salvation in Christ did not involve man's whole existence, down to his very roots.

In such a perspective the apostolate is at the service of a work of reparation, its aim being to distribute the forgiveness obtained by Christ, to restore the work disturbed by sin. Since it cannot reach man at his roots, neither can the ministry involve the Apostle in his most personal existence: he can be no more than a means for the distribution of forgiveness and grace.

All reflection on the apostolate comes up against this problem of the relations between creation and redemption, human values and Christian values. Numerous questions arise, the most insistent being undoubtedly that of the salvation of human beings who are not touched by the Church's preaching. In order to answer this question theology must start by trying to rise to as accurate as possible an appreciation of these relations. According to Vatican II, Christ's salvation, mediated by the Church, involves the whole man, "man himself, whole and entire"; the council thinks that "only in the mystery of the incarnate Word does the mystery of man take on light" and, to prove this, quotes a Pauline text (Col 1:15) which places man's creation within the mystery of Christ. (*Pastoral Constitution on the Church in the Modern World.*)

1. *God Creates in Christ*

From his conversion onwards, St Paul never stopped proclaiming Christ the Lord. At Colossae strange doctrines were trying to gain ground at the expense of this unique lordship, placing between God and mediating "powers", "thrones" and "principalities", to which homage had to be paid by "self-abasement" (Col 2:18). In the face of these theories, the Apostle reasserts the redemptive lordship of Christ, proving that it is unique and absolute, that it extends to the very origin of things and to the dawn of history, for

Creation and the Apostolate

it is the lordship of God himself who, in Christ, creates the world (Col 1:13–20):

13 He has delivered us from the dominion of darkness and transferred us to the kingdom of his beloved Son,
> 14 in whom we have redemption, the forgiveness of sins.

>> 15 He is the image of the invisible God,
>> the first-born of all creation;
>>> 16 for in him all things were created,
>>> in heaven and on earth,
>>> visible and invisible,
>>> whether thrones or dominions or principalities or authorities—
>> all things were created through him and for him.
>>> 17 He is before all things and in him all things hold together.
>>> 18 He is the head of the body, the Church;

> he is the beginning,
> the first-born from the dead,
>> that in everything he might be pre-eminent.
>>> 19 For in him all the fullness of God was pleased to dwell,
>>> 20 and through him to reconcile to himself all things,
>>> whether on earth or in heaven,
>>> making peace by the blood of his cross.

Theologians Today: F. X. Durrwell

A question arises: who is this beloved Son, for whom the Apostle claims such an absolute pre-eminence in the work of creation as well as in that of the redemption? Is he the uncreated Word, considered apart from the incarnation, or in fact Christ, the man who is Son of God, the incarnate Word?

The reply seems obvious: when the Son of God entered history, creation had been completed and in fact a long time before: he could therefore have played the creative role attributed to him by the Apostle only in his eternal existence, *outside* the mystery of the incarnation. The work of the redemption, however, belongs to the Son of God in his human existence. To the Word then belongs creative action, to Christ—that is, to the incarnate Word redemptive. This division of roles also seems to be suggested by the division of the text into two strophes, the first extolling principally the creative action of the Son of God and the other principally his work of redemption.

But this interpretation is demanded only by theological reasoning: it is based on the impossibility of Christ's exercising an activity prior to his historical existence. Scripture however must be interpreted, not in the light of theology, but in its own light: it is Scripture that is the source of theology and, in order to understand it, the only decisive criterion is the text itself, read in its context and in the faith of the Church.

The "beloved Son" is Christ. It has often been

Creation and the Apostolate

observed that, in St Paul, the Son of God and his action are never considered apart from his revelation to the world by the incarnation. There are moreover several other Pauline texts which attribute to Christ an action in the world prior to his entry into history: "the Rock (at Horeb) was Christ' (1 Cor 10:4): already, at the time of the exodus, Christ played the part of the rock of Israel. "The Lord", against whom the Israelites murmured (1 Cor 10:9), seems in fact in St Paul's thought to be the same Christ. Finally, in 1 Corinthians 8:6, the Apostle explicitly attributes to Christ a role in creation: "one Lord, Jesus Christ, through whom are all things and through whom we exist." There is then a context which justifies us in attributing to Christ a role in creation. As for the text itself, it contains evidence clear enough to make exegetes increasingly to interpret it as a whole with reference to Christ.

The two strophes are introduced by verses 13 and 14 and remain closely linked to these; the sole subject of attribution of the roles of creator and redeemer is this "beloved Son, in whom we have redemption, the forgiveness of sins"; it is he, this Son who is saviour, who "is the image of the invisible God, in whom all things were created, who is the head of the body, the first-born from the dead". The thought of the author goes back, without a break, from Christ the saviour to Christ the creator.

The beloved Son, in whom everything is created, is *the image of the invisible God* (verse 15). In Paul's eyes God dwells in inaccessible light (1 Tim 6:16;

cf. Jn 1:18); he emerges from this impenetrability, unveils his face, only in Christ. On the Damascus road Paul came to know this God whom he had not hitherto known in all his truth: he recognized him as the Father of our Lord Jesus Christ. The scales fell, his eyes were opened as he turned towards the Christ of glory (cf. 2 Cor 3:16–18). It is always Christ who is the revelation of the invisible God, the divine countenance shown to men. "The knowledge of the glory of God" is read "in the face of Christ" (2 Cor 4:6); the Christian gazes "with uncovered face on the 'glory of the Lord' (Jesus), the image *par excellence*" (2 Cor 3:18). The "earthly man" already was created in the likeness of God (Gen 1:26–28), but the "heavenly man", Christ, is "the likeness of God" (2 Cor 4:4) in its transcendent perfection. Wishing to "renew us after the image of our creator" (Col 3:10), it is in the likeness of Christ that God predestines us (Rom 8:29).

The text speaks of the "beloved Son, in whom we have redemption, *who* is the image of the invisible God"; the Pauline theology of Christ as image of God requires us to give this relative pronoun its full significance: the image of the invisible God is this Christ in whom we have redemption. This beloved Son is also *"the first-born of all creation"*. The Apostle does not say "the first-born before all creation": he places him in some way at the beginning of creation and within creation.

It would be going too far to say that the text can refer only to the man Jesus, that it is "impossible not to make the first-born the first in a series, as it is written in Romans: 'the first-born among many brethren'." The first-born of all creation is a being outside any series: he is first because "in him all things were created"; in the transcendent act of God, in which he takes part, he is "before" and above creation. And yet he is not unrelated to it, he is tied to creation by the very priority he has over it. It seems in fact that the Apostle—the Pauline perspective is one thing, that of the fourth gospel another—knows the Son of God only by his intervention in the work of God, both creative and redemptive. In order to appreciate the complexity of this thought, it seems we must understand the Son who is "first-born of all creation" not only as a man and not only as God, but as the Son who is the "image of the invisible God". In this sense he is the incomparable image and the first-born of creation both by his transcendence and by his immersion into our world.

Again it is said of this beloved Son: "all things were created through him and for him" (verse 16). The splendour of this and similar assertions might seem incompatible with the reality of the incarnation. But is it any easier to refer them to the Word apart from the mystery of the Incarnation? We can understand that everything was created by the Word, but it would be difficult to see that everything was created for him: by what title would the Word within the Trinity be the special term of creation? On the other hand, there is nothing to be said against the creation of all things for Christ, in whom the world is recapitulated, is completed and finds its unity; moreover the two epistles to the Colossians and Ephesians assert this: "He has made known to us the mystery of his will, according to his purpose which he set forth in Christ, . . . to unite all things in him" (Eph 1:9–10; cf. Col 1:20).

We can understand likewise that all things were "created in Christ" (verse 16), if it is true, as the Apostle will claim (Col 1:19; 2:9), that God has concentrated in him the "fullness" of all reality and all the divine forces of creation and sanctification. If all reality is concentrated in him, all is created in him, as a participation in his fullness.

From verse 18 onwards there can be no doubt that the text is concerned with the redeeming Christ. The part played by "the first-born from the dead", head of the Church, reconciler of all parts of the world, is again of the cosmic order. The creative sweep of his action, described in the first part, is not reduced. The dominion over death that is proper to the redeeming Christ (verse 18), according to Pauline thought, belongs to the cosmic order (cf. Phil 3:21); the reconciliation of all things in the blood of the cross belongs also to this order; the pre-eminence over the church (verse 18) is not merely juridical or imposed by external force, as are earthly sovereignties: Christ exercises his dominion over the Church as God does, in virtue of the divine fullness imparted to him (verse 19), a fullness which confers on him God's sovereignty over the universe (cf. Eph 1:19–23). But henceforward the work of creation is no longer described in its origin, as in the first strophe, but at the eschatological culmination to which "the blood of the cross" raises it.

The beloved Son is the Christ of glory. We shall be less surprised at Paul's saying that everything is created in Christ, who "is before all things", if we remember that Christ is seen, not in his earthly existence, but in his eternal fullness of glory. It is this Christ whom Paul encountered on the Damascus road, it is he who becomes for the Apostle the source of his knowledge of the world and of history (cf. 2 Cor 5:16). Everything in our text speaks of the lordly glory of the risen one: the kingdom of light into which we have been transferred (verse 13), the salvation and forgiveness that we have forever "in him" (verse 14), and, above all, this radiant image of the invisible God that is precisely the Christ of glory: "the gospel of the glory of Christ, who is the likeness of God" (1 Cor 4:4). In what follows the Apostle clearly directs our attention to Christ's resurrection: "He is the head of the body, . . . the first-born from the dead" (verse 18). According to Ephesians 1:19–23, Christ in his glorification is raised to the pinnacle of the universe, he is Lord of these same powers and principalities which the Epistle to the Colossians also shows to be subject to Christ.

St Paul provides the decisive reason for the preeminence of Christ over the church and the world: "For in him all the fullness of God was pleased to dwell" (verse 19). This word "pleroma" describes the totality of power, creative and sanctifying, and undoubtedly also the totality of being that is in God and through him in the universe. God concentrated this totality in Christ, even in his body of glory (Col 2:9), when he gave him his own name which is above all things, raising him to the plane of his being and his action, to where God is Lord (Phil 2:9-11). But God's dominion is absolute, since it is creative. This presence of the pleroma justifies the attribution to Christ of a cosmic role. For if the fullness is in him, any participation can depend only on him. The priority over all things—"he is before all things"—which creates so strange a problem for our way of thinking, is a logical consequence of the presence of the pleroma in Christ: the fullness always comes first, preceding all participation.

If theologians thought they had to deny Christ a cosmic role, it was because they ignored the incomparable glory which Scripture perceives in Christ in his resurrection. This participation in creation is an indubitably divine prerogative; but in his glorification Christ is wholly and entirely divine. What is incomprehensible is not primarily this creative role, but this pleroma of the risen Christ, the conferring of the "Name" which is nothing other than the lordship of God granted to Christ and which is exercised on the existence of things. There lies the unfathomable mystery: in the incarnation of God, in Christ's total union with God. The rest, the creative role, is the result of this. Raised to the pinnacle of all things, to the heights of God, Christ necessarily descends to the

Creation and the Apostolate

ultimate origin of things, which are all made for him (Eph 4:9ff.).

The beloved Son is the eschatological Christ. But of all this lordship, so strikingly asserted, we can say—not without regret—with the author of the Epistle to the Hebrews (2:8): "As it is, we do not yet see everything in subjection to him." In the Epistles to the Colossians and Ephesians the Apostle's vision becomes prophetic: it grasps the world's realities in their source, in the Christ of glory, in whom God at one stroke realized all the ultimate perfection of the world and completed the whole cosmic revolution, when he made dwell in him that fullness outside which nothing exists.

The subjection of the universe to Christ is not completed in the course of history, nor are all things reconciled in him. How many cracks there are in the world, how many scattered fragments! The world is created for Christ, but has not yet reached his level. The great epistles—more sensitive than those of the captivity to the slow processes of history—promise universal submission and pacification only for the last day (1 Cor 15:24–28). But they are already present in their source, the final reality is already accomplished in Christ, the eschatological resurrection is total in him who henceforward is the perfect image of God. Facing him is a world as yet only in partial union with the fullness.

The dominion of Christ is both exchatological and paschal. His glorification has made him master of the last day, "the last Adam", "the heavenly man" who comes at the end and who must renew the world (1 Cor 15:45–49). His precedence therefore is not related to the duration of the world; he entered late into history; in his glorification he is even the last, the term of a history of which he is the origin. He is first in as much as he is last, the transcendent fullness in which all things begin and end, the Alpha and the Omega (Rev 1:17; 22:13).

2. *The Connections between Creation and Redemption*
In the light of this great Scripture text, we must now try to define the mutual connections between the first creation of man and his salvation realized in Christ.

The creation of the world begins with its term. If Christ is at the origin of everything because he is its ultimate fullness, the basis and centre of humanity must be in its zenith that is to come; things and the sequence of time must be dependent on their term, in which they find fulfilment and unity; nothing will make sense or be completely intelligible except in this final realization. Any Christian reflection on man and his destiny therefore must be first of all eschatological, must try to find in the light of the end the explanation of the beginning and of the whole: this is the trend of the Apostle's thought, starting from the final redemption in order to go back to the origin.

If we want to understand the mystery of the creative act, we must see it as a creative call, as an effective attraction to ultimate fullness. As St John puts it, Christ's dominion will be imposed by

Creation and the Apostolate

attraction: "When I am lifted up from the earth—on the cross and in glory, where Christ exercises his divine prerogatives (Jn 8:28)—I will draw all men (or everything) to myself" (12:32).

This is why earthly things—which Scripture calls "carnal"—historically precede the true realities, those which do not fail, which are called "spiritual": "It is not the spiritual which is first but the physical, and then the spiritual" (1 Cor 15:46). The history of salvation proceeds from the flesh to the spirit, from man created as "a living being" (1 Cor 15:45)—therefore not in a fullness of humanity and of grace—it proceeds towards the Christ of glory who is "the Spirit" (2 Cor 3:17), reality in its divine fullness. This again is why the "carnal" realities announce the necessary advent of the realities of the spirit: "If there is a physical body, there is (then) also a spiritual body" (1 Cor 15:44); for the imperfect realities exist in virtue of a fullness that is to come. As the Apostle sees them, all the realities of the Old Testament are the shadow cast before, going back to the origins of the world, of a body to come: "These are only a shadow of what is to come; but the substance (which casts this shadow) belongs to Christ" (Col 2:17). If the shadow exists, the body that casts it exists also and its existence is more real (cf. also Eph 5:32). This is why finally the human race is *one*, radically one. Beginning with a first man in the past, mankind could only go on dispersing indefinitely, but in the Christ to come it finds not only its source, but the universal point of its convergence.

Theologians Today: F. X. Durrwell

It seems then that a Christian theology which takes up again the thought of the Old Testament in the light of Christ cannot place paradise and original justice solely at the first entry of mankind into history. For the ancient mentality which attributed power over the world to God alone, creation had to emerge finished and perfect from the hands of the creator. Man in the past therefore tended to place at the origin of things that which he made the object of his aspirations: man's complete rectitude, paradisal happiness, the golden age of humanity. Modern man cannot accept perspectives like these, since he thinks he knows through the sciences of pre-history the original precariousness of the human condition, believes in evolution and wants to contribute to the construction of the world. The Christian too, trying to understand the history of the world through faith in the incarnation and in the light of such texts as Colossians 1:15–20, finds it scarcely possible to place paradisal perfection at the origins of mankind. St Paul set himself the task of giving a Christian meaning to the Old Testament (2 Cor 3:15–17): he knew that the second Adam "became a life-giving spirit", while the first had been created only as "a living being" (1 Cor 15:45); that perfection belongs not to the beginning, but to the term. Man will therefore find paradise at the end, at the point where creation is completed, "in the heavenly places (that is) in Christ Jesus" (Eph 2:6); there too is found original justice, that of Christ, towards which he must climb.

Nevertheless, this justice is original also in time:

the history of men begins in paradise. For, from the beginning, man was created for the fullness which is in Christ, for a total communion with God: he is created therefore in an original justice and from that time onwards an inhabitant of the future paradise where he is a son of God.

Creation is a filial reality. "In him all things were created", in Christ's power as Lord, in his radiant glory as image of God. But this power and this glory are proper to him as the beloved Son, as begotten by the Father. The glorification of Jesus is nothing other than the mystery of sonship in its full realization: "This he has fulfilled in raising Jesus, as it is written, 'Thou art my Son, today, I have begotten thee'" (Acts 13:33). His power is that of his sonship: "Son of God in power by his resurrection" (Rom 1:4). It is in begetting Christ that God gives him this role in the world, that he acts in him on the world, for "whatever the Father gives the Son, he gives by begetting him". (St Augustine.)

The creation of the world thus prolongs the mystery of the incarnation. God creates when he begets his Son, Christ: he creates from this generation onwards, beginning with the image of himself that is Christ, a divine begetting which is simultaneously the dawn of creation. In his humanity Christ is the primordial creature of a world which—beginning with him—becomes in a sense wholly and entirely filial. It is therefore possible for man to find God within this world—the wisdom books and St

Paul say so—to find him, not only with the aid of laborious reasoning, but in contemplating the world, its beauty, its grandeur, in this "smile of God through the world", the radiance of the mystery of the incarnation.

Of man above all, and of every man, it can be said that he leads—up to a point—a filial life, on condition that he lives in conformity with God's creative plan: *immortal* son of God, because he lives by the Son of God raised up forever; immortal therefore in himself, since he is created in the risen Christ and for him, and again immortal by the resurrection of Christ.

To the extent to which creation is filial, not perverted by sin, it is also God's word, the expression of his being, of his plan and of what he wills. It is the fullness itself of the word in him who is at its culmination and at its origin. It is therefore essential for the Church to know this world with its aspirations and its longings which are a language of God. We must consider the world, inasmuch as it is human, with the utmost goodwill: for it is a prophecy and the remote preparation for the gace with which it is itself laden.

A world created within the redemption. If God creates us in the Christ of glory, we must conclude that he has only one plan both creative and redemptive: it must mean that God creates man within the mystery of the redemption. For, as revealed in Scripture, Christ is essentially the Saviour, Son of God for the

Creation and the Apostolate

salvation of men, "raised up for us" in his redemptive death. It is in his glory as Saviour that he is the image of God in which all is created and the pleroma in which everything subsists.

In some way therefore man is Christian at the level of his creation: his opening to God's creative action is already at least an initial opening to Christ and to final salvation; every authentic human value bears the imprint of the salvation which is in Christ, everything being created in Christ and for him. *Anima naturaliter christiana.* To be created is to be called to Christ. Once again, therefore, man is already saved in some way at the level of his human existence, being created in the Christ of glory, salvation of the world. The universal salvific will of God is written into human reality. God is (in all senses) the supreme realist, his plan of salvation is a will that becomes reality.

In this perspective, the relations between nature and grace may be understood in this way: in the concrete, there is no such thing as a state of pure nature, man is created for his supernatural end. "Nature" is man as he can be conceived when we abstract from the attraction exercised by God to draw him to this end. It is Christ who is the supernatural element in the world, Son of God in the Holy Spirit; the supernatural element is also the attraction exercised by God, drawing man to Christ. Of himself man cannot be saved, it is by creation for the fullness that he will be saved. Of himself he has no right to salvation: to be created is something to which he has no right and the more elevated is the creative action, so much the greater is its gratuitousness.

For man to fail to be saved therefore, he would have to get out of this plan, he would have to get out of it by refusing the salvation for which he is created.

Certainly men must use the means ordained for salvation. Nevertheless, they will not fail to be saved if these means are lacking, but only if they refuse them. God has revealed what man must do to be saved: he must give his faith. But God has not revealed what he will do himself for those who die before they possess the ordinary means of reaching faith. Even before they are able to seek God, men are sought by him in Christ; they will not fail to be saved unless they leave the order of salvation—that is to say, through their own fault.

It is true that mankind became sinful from the beginning and that each man belongs from birth to this sinful humanity. But sin *super*vened, came on top; it affects man at the second stage of his existence, in his belonging to other men. It affects him very deeply, in his very nature, for he would not be truly man apart from this belonging to other men. And yet man belongs to the second Adam, his saviour, more radically than to the first. Before he is a member of a sinful community, he is created by God and for Christ. It can even be said that forgiveness of sins comes first, it is sufficient for man unceasingly to accept this.

Since everything is created in the saving lordship of Christ, earthly realities too *can* be bearers of

Creation and the Apostolate

salvation for us; all events *can* be referred to the great event, the death and resurrection of Christ. Even before they know Christ, men help one another on the way of salvation, if they help one another to be truly human. In order to understand better the truths of salvation revealed to it, the Church must also listen to the world in which the leaven of salvation is already at work.

What is more, human beings on earth are all in some way members of the Church, to the extent that they accept the creative plan of God. They belong to the Church by their roots, these roots of their being by which they live already on their future, Christ, for whom they are created.

For the Church, in the world, is the sacrament of the presence and action of Christ by which the world is and must become filial. Having realized the pleroma in Christ, God fills up the Church with this fullness (Col 2:9) to the point at which it becomes in its turn the pleroma, the very body of Christ (Col 1:18; Eph 1:23), the sacrament for men of their creation in Christ: "(God) has made (Christ) the head over all things for the Church, which is his body, the fullness of him (Christ) who fills all in all."

In its mystery the Church is the culmination of humanity within the world, a culmination not yet attained by the rest of the world, but already immanent in it by the action of God who creates humanity for the redeeming Christ. The Church is not apart because of its election; it is built at the heart of the city of men. Among men it constitutes the narrowest circle in which Christ is present to all mankind and acts upon it. From this fullness outwards the grace of God seeks to spread to all men. The Church is not only the symbol of the world's salvation, but also the leaven in the whole (Mt 13:33), the leaven which must gradually penetrate everywhere; this it is by its testimony and teaching and first of all by its presence at the heart of mankind with Christ whose body it is. The communion of saints spreads its light beyond the Church of faith and the sacraments, as the action of Christ itself, towards all men right back to the origins of history, towards all men around it in space, who do not knowingly and effectively cut themselves off from it. The axiom "outside the church no salvation" means, when it is positively formulated, that the Church and the Church alone in the world is the source of salvation for all men of good will. When therefore Christians go out to meet other human beings in order to bring them the message of Christ and of the Church, the grace of Christ *and* of the Church will have preceded them. God's initiative in Christ and in the Church is absolute: it does not come to help man to enter into the order of salvation; it creates him within that order and directs him to salvation by way of the human reality itself. The Apostle who brings the message must therefore be attentive to the road already travelled by men, to the ecclesial values they already possess; he must respect their aspirations, the riches of civilization of a people and its religious

Creation and the Apostolate

feeling. To act otherwise would be to compromise the dynamism of the grace which has always been at work in these men's hearts directing them towards faith.

This salvation is still to be realized. Basically, men have received baptism: they are in some way Christian, in some way saved. Nevertheless, the Church would be wrong to say to itself: "Why impose on me the heavy burden of an uncertain apostolate? They are Christians, they are saved! Why provoke a crisis, making them face a decision for or against Christ and the Church, since they are already Christians even without this decision? Isn't it sufficient to help them fraternally to be human beings, simply human beings?"

From all the evidence of Scripture, salvation is not immanent in such a way that man needs only to exist and develop horizontally—so to speak—on the level at which he began to be. Salvation is at the centre of mankind, but on another level and prior to man: an inner peak which remains to be climbed. Mankind must surpass itself in order to advance towards what it is in Christ. He in whom and for whom everything *is created is the eschatological Christ*: he draws men from the height of the cross and we reach him by rising above our first state, in an "elevation above the earth". "*People are not born, but become Christians.*" (Tertullian.) The reality of salvation consists in this final reality which is Christ dead and risen: in human values it exists as yet only in the form of a more or less distant promise. Salvation is an objective to which man is called.

God creates by a call, by his creating and attracting Word, Christ dead and risen, who is salvation. Man is not already saved in what he is, but in what he becomes in Christ. If God were to refuse to bring about this becoming beyond his first state, man would not be saved. If man were to resist the process of becoming, he would cut himself off from salvation. We have said that, to fail to be saved, man would have to get out of the plan of salvation: he gets out of it when he renounces the fullness for which he never ceases to be created.

Earthly things are in some way Christian, as related to this ultimate fullness. Ambivalent in themselves, they must be surpassed in the use that is made of them. They are like the shadow cast by a body. It is possible to be attached to these things without regard to their ultimate fullness and then the shadow is taken for the reality, there is a refusal of the process of becoming, a lapse into idolatry. Man must therefore renounce himself unceasingly, undertake continually to surpass himself; he must consent to his progressive creation towards fullness. It is this going beyond oneself for the sake of fullness that scripture calls dying to "the flesh".

This dying—a total death—is written into the very term of human becoming, in Christ who is its ultimate fullness, glorified in a permanent death to "the flesh".

And this term is a *redemptive* death, proof for man of his essential need to be saved from sin. So far as

Creation and the Apostolate

he fails to share in this glorifying death, he is a sinner: he is so by the margin of shadow that encircles his earthly existence, for anyone who lacks the glorious holiness of God is a sinner (Rom 3–23); he is so even more through the sin in which the whole human community is implicated from the beginning and through his personal sins. Created for a Christ glorified in death, man has a deep-rooted need to die himself; death is part of the mystery of creation. But, as willed by God, it is a pasch, a passing, a consent to fullness.

The Church's necessary apostolate. The eschatological fullness is offered for man's consent in as much as Christ enters into the world and encounters men. He does this in the Church and through his apostolate. Since any authentic human value depends on the grace of Christ, the conclusion is sometimes drawn that every truly human being is truly a Christian, a Christian who most often is unaware of the fact and to whom the Church has the mission of revealing his Christian identity: it must place him in the presence of Christ in whom he will recognize himself. The mission of the Church, in this view, is not to bring grace, but to make people aware of its presence.

This, however, is not the Church's essential mission. It is useful for man to come to know what he is already; but what is really important is to bring into being what does not yet exist. If it had no other role than that of making men aware of a salvation already realized, the Church would not be necessary for salvation and the apostolate would be of secondary importance, for it is more important to be than to know. Although he has received much, man has much still to receive: *he still has everything to receive*, Christ, the totality of salvation.

Evangelization is the "epiphany" of the salvation to come: its revelation and its realization. Through the Church, its life and its message, the eschatological reality blazes a trail in the world, addresses its creative call to men and is imparted to them. St Paul was conscious of a cosmic mission. He knew that he was endowed with a force which is active in the glorification of Christ, the creative force of the new world. Through the apostles God pronounces the reconciling word (2 Cor 5:18–20), by which he brings back everything under one head (Eph 1:10): "to reconcile to himself all things, whether on earth or in heaven" (Col 1:20). Through the faith that the Apostles rouses, through the sacraments he celebrates, man is incorporated into the body of Christ where the creation of men is begun and completed.

The duty of believing the Apostle. It is not easy to believe in the mission of the Church, in this power with which it is invested to perfect the creation of the world. Results which are often derisory, Christians—that is, ourselves—who are so ineffective, our evident weakness: all these make our grandiose claims seem merely the fabric of a dream. But in Christianity everything is paradoxical. There is a folly of the cross as well as faith in the cross (cf.

Creation and the Apostolate

1 Cor 1:18). Faith means sharing in the cross, and this is folly: faith is therefore folly.

Who will deny that this creative power of God is at work in the apostle if he believes that, in Christ and the Church, men become "a new creation" (2 Cor 5:17; Gal 6:15) and that the communion of saints is the new world? If we reflect on it, the very weakness of the Church makes its faith and its hopes less incredible. Everything points to the fact that the only proportion between the creative power of God and man's action on earth is an apparently inverse ratio of greatness: that power is seen to be infinite only in weakness; that wisdom is revealed as divine only under the empty appearances of faith; and eternal life is visible in the death of Christ. Man is called to rule over creation, not only by subjecting it to himself (Gen 1:26), but by participating in the divine action on the world. This participation is most intense in the Church, destined to lead the world to its final perfection; it is therefore normal for the Church to resemble him who is the perfect image of God in his creative action: Christ in the mystery of his pasch.

DATE DUE			
GAYLORD			PRINTED IN U.S.A.